South Croxted

South Croxted

MARTIN RICHARDSON

Atara Press

Copyright © 2012 by Martin Richardson
Published by Atara Press, Los Angeles. www.atarapress.com
British Library Cataloguing in Publication Data
A catalogue record for this book is available from the British Library

All images from the personal archive of Martin Richardson except as noted.
Jacket design by Andersen M Studio.
Text set in Monotype Dante 11.25 pt.

ISBN: 978-0-9822251-7-2

Paper sourced from environmentally aware forest product companies.
EDITIONS PRINTED IN THE UNITED KINGDOM AND THE UNITED STATES

Contents

Time – He's waiting in the wings
He speaks of senseless things
His script is you and me…

"Time" DAVID BOWIE

AUTHOR'S NOTE

WHEN I WAS A CHILD, my father told me that the engineers who built the subway in Victoria encountered problems with a vast underground network of rivers, such as the Fleet and tributaries flowing from the nearby Thames. The complex coverage of deep shafts remained unseen by human eye until the Second World War when falling German bombs cracked open vast cave entrances to expose virtually bottomless holes stretching from Highgate Cemetery in the North, to Billingsgate Fish Market in the East. The deepest was to be found directly under the Bank of England and that's where all the dirty money ended up. Even today I still listen for running torrents of water when I stand at the far end of the southbound platform on the Victoria line, despite knowing my father's story to be untrue...

Dedicated to Lizzie & Flo

Brixton Fog 1958

A THICK, CHOKING FIFTY-MILE BELT of industrial smog descended over London's metropolis and seeped into the back rooms of the poor slums of Brixton. Electric Avenue's busy, bustling market with its vast range of food and clothes stores, many of African origin, came to a standstill. Food markets outside the British Rail station on Atlantic Road, running through Electric Avenue, had prospered from the recent huge wave of West Indian immigration brought by the Windrush journey to Britain. These market stalls were an important focal point for the black community, serving up specialities such as flying fish, breadfruit and all manner of weird-looking fresh meats, even Nigerian monkey flesh. Electric Avenue, the original South London market, is protected by extended awnings that run the length of the street; huge sheets of glass that seemingly hover above the pavement to protect both pedestrians and stall traders from the rain. It gained fame as the first street in Britain to be lit entirely by electricity in 1860. The shops, with their tall, fancy terraces suggestive of dreams, are a fashionable retail haunt. But this vicious three-dimensional yellow smog diffused the electric incandescent light of the avenue to little more than a dim glow from a burning candle.

Not all white Britons welcomed the migrants and many West Indians found the colour of their skin provoked unfriendly reactions. Despite the desperate shortage of labour, some still found it difficult to get good jobs. They were often forced to accept work that they were overqualified for, or were paid less than white workers. Since few had money, they had to find cheap housing to rent near to their workplace. This was often in the poor inner cities. Even if they did have enough money to rent better quality housing, many had to face the fact that some landlords refused to rent to black people, who found themselves confronted with discriminating signs in windows that read: *Room To Let: No Dogs, No Irish, No Coloureds.*

As the damp October pea soup smog descended to street level, many were ready for it. Out came the cloth masks they had bought earlier in the week after the radio had broadcast a public health warning. All over the capital, chemists had reported a big demand for the masks which, said the doctors, could help prevent a disaster similar to that of the previous October, when smog had reaped a heavy death toll. The atmospheric of lethal smog had gripped Eastern England from Yorkshire to London and Blackheath in South London, where the dense mist gave an otherworldliness to the mass burial graveyard of the unfortunate victims of the 1665 Great Plague.

Smog reports were sent out from the city, where a Ministry of Health official announced that the government was "working to produce a better mask," as had been suggested by London's doctors and a highly qualified scientist had been engaged several months earlier to work on the problem, but no details of the new experimental mask were yet available. By early evening, London and Northolt airports were completely blacked out. Incoming flights from Paris and Brussels were directed to Blackbushe Airport, and long distance services from as far away as the Mediterranean were held up in Paris, all outgoing planes having returned to hangers. Brixton came to a standstill as vehicles mounted pavements in the impenetrable gloom and drivers lost their way. Most people stayed at home; cinemas and theatres were half empty. This was South London 1958, emerging from the bleak period of post-war austerity, a place where fantasy and violence merged to constitute an unearthly uncertainty.

Victor was returning home from Victoria by a bus that was forced to terminate in Brixton due to the appalling visibility. Vagrants had set up make-shift camps just under the railway entrance where, arms outstretched, they begged pennies from those stranded in the fog. As Victor passed, he flicked a silver shilling above their heads to tease the wretched souls, until it bounced from the metal-rimmed steps of the station exit and fell into one dirty hand.

A weathered face looked up, astonished at Victor's kindness and said in a rich Cockney accent, "Gawd bless, governor, you must be a bleedin' millionaire."

Victor smiled. Random acts of generosity reinforced a delusion that he was rich, but in truth Victor was closer to down-at-heal than he would ever admit.

It was here, in the very heart of the smog that Victor came into the presence of Samuel, a meeting that would have extraordinary and significant consequences. Samuel moved slowly through the mist, like a giant toad surfacing from the depths of a muddy pond. His thick neck supported a huge head, all topped by a gray felt fedora that gave contrast to his smooth dark brown skin like some exotic forbidden luxury. Samuel's pupils were demon-like, impenetrably black with whites the colour of custard, a symptom of long-term hepatitis. An eye in appearance, shape and relative position, but unlike any eyes Victor had ever seen before.

He asked Victor, in a deep baritone African accent, "Please, sir. Excuse me, sir, forgive me, sir, but do you have a room to rent? I have just arrived in your country from Africa and seek accommodation. I can pay, sir... Look, my friend... I am rich."

"Come on, mate, that's a bit far fetched, isn't it?" Victor replied, thinking of his own previous act of benevolence. "Prove it!" he challenged the stranger.

Samuel reached into the breast pocket of his greatcoat and produced a black velvet purse. Loosening its string he took from it a small, sparkling, blue diamond. Victor struck a match to see better and to his amazement the piece of pure compressed carbon radiated light with the brilliance of a solar flair. Like the lens of a lighthouse, it focused the light warning a dangerous coastline, warning the lost souls within the fog of danger ahead.

Victor could hardly believe his luck, then considered his good fortune. "Yes, my friend," he said, holding out his cold hand, "that will do!"

Samuel placed the blood diamond in Victor's palm and closed it, as if it were part of a conjuring trick. A deal was struck and Victor brought Samuel home.

*

By 9am the following morning, the weather had improved dramatically and the fog had lifted. This was Samuel's opportunity to see South Croxted in daylight, to examine the house. He found it unlike anything he could have ever imagined. From outward appearances, the house seemed exactly like the other late Edwardian, high-ceilinged houses that lined South Croxted. A two-storey semi-detached property of no consequence, joined on the left by its neighbour and yet there was something strange about it, something less conventional. The inlayed stained-glass panels of the front door depicted large, deep blue-coloured hearts surrounded by sapphire roses.

From certain angles, one could see the house as a skull-like face; a trick of the light shaped by shadows from the alcoves as the sun tracked the sky. The upper windows appeared as sunken eyes that gazed to the right, toward the tattooed door that appeared to be a twisted mouth, as if about to spit out something sour... something unsaid. Unlike its neighbouring houses, whose gardens were beautifully well-maintained, ours was left untended. Feral with overgrown weeds and wild roses that perennially blossomed, just as the Edwardian builder had planned. The soil in which they grew had remained neglected and untilled for many years.

Samuel's room was a dingy, damp, bedsit situated upstairs toward the back of the house. He had left his wife and six dependent children back in Africa with a dream of bringing them to England once he had settled. The lodgings were a sanctuary from an African war about to erupt in the Congo. He came from a region of the Congo called Katanga. Like one of the last remaining great silverbacks that roamed the mountain region of his beautiful country, he too was seeking protection from extinction.

He claimed to be a good man, a man of principles forced to leave his country and chiefdom in order to escape war. Paradoxically, it was the very riches of the land that were leading to its very scarcity. At night, Victor and Samuel would spend hours locked in conversation, where Samuel revealed a sinister, more disturbing, side to his personality. Victor's relationship with Samuel was defined by a commonality of violence and nowhere was more suitable for this bond than Brixton. A place impervious to reason, this undulating melting pot of the poor working class defined Victor and his playground. A place where, in the late 1950s, large numbers of immigrants arrived, but a place where outbreaks of violence against them were rare, unlike Notting Hill, where mobs of white people often attacked black people in the streets, smashing or burning their homes. It was in this community that Victor considered himself a champion of the people, for he taught English to West Indian children at the local primary school, some of whom were to lead the Brixton riots in the 1980s. Victor's teaching came to an end with my arrival when he stapled my birth certificate to the staff notice board:

RAILTON ROAD SCHOOL NOTICE BOARD
ANNOUNCEMENTS FOR OCTOBER 1958

It was evidence of his fertility, but ultimately an action that led to him being taken into custody and later imprisoned. For my birth certificate was inconsistent with other paperwork, paperwork which Victor had used to secure his job – his forged teaching certificates in which he had somehow overlooked to alter something that eagle-eyed head of maths, Mr Prime, soon brought to the attention of Dr Bead, the headmaster. Prime had long thought there was something suspect about Victor, but had had no evidence until now.

As overstretched classrooms attempted to accommodate the influx of West Indian children, the local council was desperate for staff and overlooked many of the usual crucial details. My birth certificate provided the evidence Prime sought, because on it, in the box marked *Father's Occupation*, Victor had written, *Merchant Seaman*. It also gave dates, together with other conflicting information, giving grounds for closer scrutiny. After several hours of urgent telephone calls to the authorities, it became apparent that Victor was not the teacher he had claimed to be. He wasn't even the person he claimed to be, as it also came to light that he had changed his name the year before my birth, from Biddlecome to Lionheart-Richardson. The police were called and, with much shock from legitimate members of the school staff, especially the dinner ladies who had fallen for his charm and good looks, off to Brixton police station he went for questioning, where it soon became clear Victor was a fraud and he was arrested for deception.

The judge sentenced Victor to three years' punitive correction, to be served first at Wormwood Scrubs, then HMP Ford, the open prison, also known as "Poofters Palace" for its low level security and white-collared inmates. Before he was taken from the Old Bailey, my mother and I visited him in the holding cell and sat opposite him on a bench. He was still wearing his cream flannel suit, white shirt and green-striped tie, having not yet put on his prison regulation uniform of pinstripe collarless shirt, air force grey short jacket and woollen trousers that rested on the seat next to him. The room was full of whispers. There were no smiles, only sombre, remorseful sighs and thoughts of missing love.

The tabloids had a field day with my father's story. The *Daily Express, News of The World* and even the *Daily Mirror* headlined the story: **FAKE TEACHER GOES TO GAOL**. Rattled by this disruption, Samuel made the decision to return to Africa, to redeem himself in the eyes of his people and avoid any unnecessary attention. But it wouldn't be long before the relevance of his relationship with Victor spread beyond the shores of England to become global news.

*

Victor's imprisonment didn't last long. The following summer, the parole board granted my father freedom on the grounds of good behaviour. But, on his return to Croxted Road, his violent outbursts within the intimacy of the family increased in frequency. He would perform bizarre antics such as swinging from the low branches of the cooking apple tree in the garden, flexing his adult muscles and challenging my teenaged brother Raymond to punch him as hard as he possibly could in the stomach. Raymond willingly obliged, as he loathed Victor above all else. But his blows aimed at maiming his father didn't even wind him. Without so much as the blink of an eyelid, Victor put on a real iron man display. Even when at home, my father sidestepped his identity. We were never permitted to call him Dad, for it would have identified him for who he really was, our father. He had an unrealistic psychotic view of the world, warping the real world to justify his paranoia. The bigger problems occurred when he found this impossible and unleashed his frustrations on the family, who bore the brunt of his perversities. As time passed, these distortions manifested themselves in a number of ways, including the wearing of white boiler suits during exercise and a shabby merchant seaman officer's uniform when going out. The uniform was dry-cleaned for social gatherings such as Christmas, funerals and weddings, and was worn with pristine white laundered shirts with cardboard-stiff disposable collars attached to the neck of the shirt with studs. He looked like something the war had forgotten, the final remaining soldier hiding in the Burmese jungle thirty years after, unaware the war had ended, or perhaps a lost extra from *The Sound of Music*. One Christmas, I photographed him wearing it as he replaced some fused fairy lights that hung from a sparkling, tinsel-draped, plastic Christmas tree. Later, I entered the photograph into a competition and won first prize in the "Dream" section. The judges were very complimentary, commenting how *the twinkling glow from the multi-coloured bulbs of Christmas tree lights complemented the remarkable surreal juxtaposition of combat clothing to evoke the sensation of a "Never-Never Land."*

If only they knew.

To strangers, Victor was the most charming and congenially apologetic gentleman, hiding anything he felt was unclean, any by-product of life, with a clinically compulsive cleansing and self-grooming regime. Grooming his hair to the point when his scalp would bleed, nail filing to feminine perfection, to later coat them with clear nail varnish, something quite metrosexual. Visiting the laundrette every day, only to return with other people's washing. His *raison d'être*, however, were his teeth. These were clinically cleaned every month by trainee hygienists at Guy's Dental Hospital. Ask any dentist and they will tell you about the crazy volunteer patients they have to deal with.

Victor invented illnesses and at times real ailments were self-inflicted, such as dropping heavy weights onto his feet and undergoing necessary surgery. He made his phantasms real as he studied *Gray's Anatomy* with focused intent, to feed what may have been Münchausen's Syndrome. In culmination, his self-inflected wounds would lead to hospitalisation, a physical manifestation of his own inner torment. All this made South Croxted an odd place for a child. Rather than fables at bedtime, he would tell me how horrible the world could be and what a good, misunderstood man he was. He would tell me horror stories, so I would fear the bogeyman more than him and so make me afraid of something that did not exist... something only in his mind. He warned me, "Martin, as God is my witness, if you ever mock me I will kill you!"

Like everyone else in the house, I too suffered from bad dreams as Victor's madness engulfed both day and night. At night, I would lay awake imagining Satan's face in the flowered wallpaper patterns. I convinced myself that child killers lurked in the darkness of the garden and the sound of rain gently tapping on my window was a demonic gargoyle, beckoning me to lift the curtain so I could see its horrific form to torment me further. But once asleep, I had the most beautiful dreams. There was one recurring dream that I have never forgotten...

It's a beautiful spring morning. Sunlight streams through open French doors that lead to a picturesque estate. The smell of sweet, fragrant blossom fills the cool, fresh air and dappled shadows fall from a young sapling apple tree in a garden. A round dining table stands at the end of a long room and its shining surface reflects a brilliant blue sky. A man and a woman stand next to this table, both smartly dressed in clothes that appear to date from another century. They smile at me and I feel an overwhelming sensation of love. I am looking up toward them, the view of a standing child. I suddenly recognise the man and woman from a photograph that hangs in the hallway of South Croxted. The man's bearded, distinctive profile is that of the King. The woman at his side, his Queen. It is a dream of wish fulfilment, a patchwork of positive images embedded into my thoughts forever.

Domestic life confined Victor to a very narrow space and only outside the house did the Good Samaritan figure, the teacher, emerge free to avoid family ratiocination and the realities of parenthood, larger than life but smaller than human. Victor lived in a world of avarice, where reality was twisted for personal gain without question, all sense of proportion destroyed by delusion. He entertained multiple personalities, a reverie without logic, removed from reality. He was a man who made his own true personality transparent by inventing an invisible cloak within which he lost himself; a shadow within a shadow. He despised celebrities but was desperate to be one. The true Victor was always absent and as he slid further from his true self into la-la land, he took a chunk of my childhood with him and my boundary between the real and the imagined merged. I know it's simply the cards we're dealt, but Victor cheated. He bent the rules of reality until the distortions made life itself so abstract, it became meaningless. Sadly, I cannot say that it ended well, for only three weeks after release he packed his bags, and without saying goodbye he made his way to America, to New York City.

The Kinema 1960

Blackbirds gathered high in the branches of the tall elms in Central Park to catch the last remaining rays of sunset. Warm thermal currents lifted others even higher, up beyond the condominium apartments of the successful rich, up to the height of the Empire State Building where only the strongest of birds could fly. The sound of children playing in the distance reminded Victor of his own children. He thought how swiftly time passed and how he would soon be little more than a memory to them. Life was too good to waste time thinking about such things and if he were to make the most of it, he needed money. He needed one final big deal, the deal of a lifetime.

Traffic cops whistled above the traffic roar, as the grid of sidewalks and patchy pavements became alive with makeshift kitchens serving homemade hot-dogs, or exotic fruit crushed ices served in pint-sized plastic tumblers. Small restaurants pitched their delights haphazardly between gutter and pavement, where the smell of sizzling onions and coffee overpowered the deluge of fumes from passing gas guzzlers. The huge neon lights adorning department stores such as Macy's and Bloomingdale's bedazzled him and Times Square particularly impressed, with its multi-coloured neon illumination that ran a block and a half, before petering out to the less commercial district where the sound of gunfire could be heard echoing from downtown Harlem.

Victor lifted his glass and sipped on a warm Coke. Looking through the open bedroom window from the ninth floor of the YMCA, he watched as the rush hour speeded its commute, like seething lava from a volcano.

Here's to the end of England, he thought, content with the idea that he would spend the rest of his life destroying it.

Friday evening's population was gathering as New York rushed home to watch the big game on TV. The Brooklyn Dodgers and New York Giants were playing their final season but something was haunting Victor. He couldn't get his first wife, Daphne, out of his head. The very mention of her name made my mother erupt into rage, despite his divorce from Daphne being decreed absolute five years earlier in 1956. He was struggling to pay maintenance for his son, Neil, the skeleton in the cupboard, my half brother I never met. I was his fourth child, that last shake of the bag...

As the sun fell behind the Manhattan skyline, his bearded, naked body chilled faster than the warm Coke. A million lights turned on to illuminate another world of consumerism, abstract art, power, money and mystery. In the midst of plenty, Victor felt empty. As tenants returned home from work, he watched the incandescent bulbs turn on to illuminate apartment after apartment in a surge of power unlike anything he had ever seen before. The failing light gave way to the image of his reflection in the building opposite. A city of reflection upon reflection, concealing the activity of what lay behind. His naked, mirrored image watched as the warm American sun set on the horizon, to rise in London, where daybreak seemed something of a novelty without him. Victor sat on the edge of his bed and fathomed the wealth of New York City. *What a phenomenal asset,* he thought. *To imagine such huge amounts of money is quite bewildering. If only I could have a piece...*

With only a few dollars left to his name, less then half the overdue rent, he decided to go and see a movie, get out and live a little. The soft mattress retained the shape of his delicate, unconscious body long after he had risen, the shape of a dream, cast as an imprint central to the bedroom. Bubonic blisters spoilt the decorative plastic surface of the bedside cabinet where cigarettes had been left to smoulder and burn in circular patterns around the ash tray. The Essential Gideon Bible lay open in the top draw with well-thumbed pages of a parable that asked for strength, and where someone had scribbled an adage in pencil that read, *Everything we are doing, or have ever done, will be forgotten in the Alzheimer's of time...* biblical graffiti.

Across the street on Broadway, a cinema was showing H. G. Wells' *The Time Machine* where extras wearing blond wigs act out the part of the beautiful Eloi race while midgets dressed in pallid green, ill-fitting costumes portray the glow-eyed subterranean Morlock freaks. They sneak out from behind painted paper boulders to capture the time machine and the man who had travelled to our future from the past expecting to find an advanced civilisation, but instead found a world full of man-eating cannibals and idiot quarry. In the best scene, they get a thrashing from the handsome, physically perfect actor Rod Tailor who went on to star as the voice of Pongo the Dalmatian in Disney's animated *One Hundred and One Dalmatians*.

As he lay restless that night the sound coming out from the neighbouring room was disturbing. Even with the television volume turned up high, the thin walls echoed with a deep bellowing voice that demanded money:

"I want you to make me billions of dollars, do you hear me? Billions, not millions. My father had to work hard for our people like you and he got nothing in return – now it's your turn to work hard for me. Move your arse over here so I can take what rightfully belongs to me and you get what you deserve. Bend over."

An hour later the door opened then slammed shut. He got out of bed and pressed his eye to the spy-glass to see the distorted shape of two excited young men running around the hallway, giggling and playing like children, even though they must have been in their twenties. They picked handfuls of sweets from the complimentary candy bowl in the corridor and started throwing them at each other in a game of fast catch with voices muffled in a silent excited whine, like children who had just seen Santa Claus and didn't want to wake their parents in an excited game of delight. The long hallway of the hotel made for the perfect 100-metre track, so long as no one left the safety of their room to collide with the speeding resident athletes.

The hairdresser on the ground floor lobby ran a shop called *The Pussycat Doll*. Inside a group of middle-aged women were opening bottles of Californian white wine and had decided to have a drunken hairdressing competition. They giggled as they backcombed, broke wind and coughed chesty coughs simultaneously. A vision not lost on the hotel doorman who eavesdropped and belly rocked in amusement.

"Gorgeous! Look at that, come on Suzy…let everyone admire your hair. Don't you see honey? It was hard before – now it's all lovely and soft. Remember your fringe? Well we got rid of that so you look sixteen again."

"What, you mean sixteen stone?" said another as they screamed with laughter. The picture of hilarity was something quite wholesome, somehow normal.

As Victor left his room so too did the voice from next door. A man had great stature, smartly dressed in a pin-striped business suit and polished shoes. They entered the elevator together and Victor nodded hello.

"Good evening, sir!" said the man as the doors slid to close.

It was one of life's awkward moments as Victor looked into the elevator mirror and noticed the man staring at him from the corner of his eye. Victor decided it best not to acknowledge him further and was quite relieved as the elevator doors opened at ground level and the man gestured with an outstretched his arm.

"After you, sir."

"Why thank you!" Victor replied and made his way past The Pussycat Doll hairdressers, through the revolving doors and into the street beyond. Victor could only imagine what the man had been up to, but whatever it was, it was something to be avoided.

Victor wanted to explore the relentless roar of industrial New York and escape thoughts of responsibility. He needed to find a job. America had no social welfare, a thought that made him feel homesick. That, and being away from his mother, caused an unpleasant taste at the back of his throat that he found hard to swallow. He walked from the YMCA to Mercer Street, then into Central Park where he strolled a voyeuristic landscape of voluptuous extremes. He saw the hookers congregating behind bushes, displaying nature's goods as their pounding bangles made a rhythmic beat to milk the lonely men who mistook prostitution for love. Others walked in a ritual circle displaying slender figures, maintained by drug abuse rather than diet, as if they were livestock in a meat market. They cried:

"Want some love, babe? Five bucks a hand job, blow job fifteen," and a steady flow of men appeared as if carried by an invisible lust escalator from hell and darkness.

A cardboard cut-out from the Japanese Tourist Agency stood on the reception desk in the lobby of the YMCA. Its image of cherry trees in full pink blossom, together with a young couple walking hand in hand, portrayed an image of naivety. A small narrow-gauge railway receded into the distance towards snow-capped scenery of Mt. Fuji. Japan was recovering from the atomic bombs of Hiroshima and Nagasaki, and strived to portray a country now living in harmony with Nature, but Nature is not as predictable as the printed cardboard would have us believe. Like the couple in the cardboard advert, Victor had come to New York in the pursuit of happiness and a perfect world. He longed for things not yet achieved, and to escape the things he had failed at. America promised everything he ever wanted. It was his *West Side Story*, but that night the Brixton Ritzy and Leonard Bernstein seemed little more than a distant memory as the smell of sweet caramel lingered in the warm evening air, moving through a thousand open windows lit by the blue lights from bug zappers, and street traders make their last sale of the day before going home to feed their salivating children.

Victor found a job eventually as a train attendant for Amtrak Services on the East Coast route, New York to Boston. His English accent made him a popular minor celebrity and he felt at home with his fellow workers, mainly black, from the Bronx or Harlem. They liked him, they all knew someone or had West Indian relatives in Brixton. These hard-working men were what the whites referred to as "coloured waiters," and although segregation was being highlighted by the likes of Martin Luther King, it was still accepted.

The impressive railcars were enormous in every sense; the height of a London double-decker and stretched a mile. All was well until the day he was asked to wait on a table occupied by the Hollywood movie star Yul Brynner who had leapt to fame as a result of his starring role in *The King and I.* Now Brynner was on a publicity tour for his cowboy movie, *The Magnificent Seven.* While Victor was serving the soup to Brynner, he tripped and sent the consommé flying over Brynner's bald head. Needles to say, Victor faced immediate dismissal. As the train reached Central Station that evening, he stole a set of silver salt and pepper dispensers when no one was looking, despite the fact they had been embossed, *Property of Amtrak.*

What a nice gift these will make for someone, he thought, and walked away without so much as a goodbye.

That night, he made his way to the public library which remained open until nine o'clock and searched through the shipping listings and shipping agents. He identified three within walking distance of the harbour before making his way back to the YMCA by taxi. On arrival, he went through the pretence of searching for change in his suit pockets before asking the driver to wait a few moments whilst he collected the fare from a friend, then ran in the opposite direction and down into the subway to avoid payment.

"You fucking jerk!" yelled the cab driver, deciding there and then never to be polite to a "Limey arsehole" again.

One address Victor found in the listings directory provided employment at Seatankers Inc, located at 380 Madison Avenue and the following morning, he presented himself as a fresh-faced radio officer ready for duty. He was offered a job as a crew member on board the freighter *S.S. William R. Folbert,* destined for Cuba to collect a shipment of cigars and sugar cane. This was two years before such voyages were banned due to the Cuban missile crises. The ships operated by Seatankers Inc used skeleton crews, as far too many of their cargos were considered dangerous, making insurance premiums for normal crews unacceptable. Instead, they paid employees handsomely for putting their lives at risk. Before leaving New York, Victor sent photographs of himself posing in Central Park back home to his doting mother, while Stella received a single flimsy acetate recorded disc. It was a recording of his voice made at the amusement park on Coney Island, a recording I would often play when alone as a child and it haunts me to this day.

He talks…

"There is a name for this situation, this problem. I can't think of it at the moment but it will come. I have no idea of where I am. Who I am, or rather who I have become, is not important. What is important is that you understand how I became that person…"

It was only a sentence, a few words, but I felt as if his soul talked directly to me, as if a pallid blue ectoplasm rose from the disc as it revolved at 78rpm to engulf me in its vapour and pull me in toward its spiralling centre, towards its black swallowing darkness.

★

30,000 nautical miles later and after six months at sea, Victor returned to South Croxted. His boredom with being aquatic had removed any contempt he had for England. Apart from the inclement weather that always seemed cold, damp and wet, he felt pleased to be back and was amused by how much the children had grown. It was during this period of relative calm that one afternoon, he took shelter from the rain in a small cinema located above platform 17 at Victoria Station.

The cinema was a remnant from World War Two, built for troops awaiting trains that would take them on to the front line. That afternoon, it was screening a black and white newsreel about an African crisis that was turning into a multi-national war on the other side of the world. The newsreel was titled *The Belgian Congo Affair*. Through the blue haze of cigarette smoke, Victor watched the flickering newsreel with great interest as its image beamed above the heads of the spectators, forming long, thin spikes of weightless abstract shapes in the haze.

The Kinema, as it was called, screened *Looney Tunes* cartoons and *British Pathé News* features during the day, then at night, after the respectable rush of suburban commuters had returned home, hard-core Swedish blue movies. The 1960s focus on free love and hippies, rapid and radical change, was complementary to the adult indulgences that Maurice, the owner of The Kinema, supplied. This earned him the title of "The Porno King." Maurice was an overweight, ruined playboy with sleepy eyes framed by deep wrinkles from too many late nights of self-abuse. He was a man with a penchant for kinky stuff, such as bondage and masochism, so when The Obscene Publications Act came into force in 1959, he seized the opportunity to profit from it, justifying its exploitation in the name of freedom. The cinema offered men a place to escape thoughts of war and destruction, a place to masturbate, to live out fantasy.

How ludicrous, Victor thought, *if Samuel's image were to appear on the screen, and how nice it would be to see him again.* Samuel had returned to the Katanga region of Africa and had become embroiled in the political struggle of the newly formed Independent Democratic Republic of the Congo. In fact, he had become a key figure, leading the revolt against the western-backed government of President Patrice Lumumba in the place featured on the newsreel.

It reported scenes of "hot war" developing in Africa…

"A place," said the voiceover of Clement Cave, the voice of British Pathé newsreel, the voice of a nation, "that urgently requires doctors."

How very nationalistic of those newly independent states, and what untapped wealth, he thought.

Africa was in turmoil. In Rhodesia, an unknown demonstrator called Nelson Mandela was on trial along with one hundred and fifty-five others, having made his famous Winds of Change speech. This was a situation that the then British Prime Minister, Harold Macmillan, likened to the…

"Break-up of the Roman Empire."

What, Victor thought, *could be more alluring than an exciting trip to the tropics?*

The newsreel continued…

"As the Cold War escalates between the superpowers, the Cuban Missile Crises and the fall of French Algeria could mean the end of our world as we know it, the utter obliteration of our planet!"

In retaliation for Cuba's relationship with the Soviet Union and its support of communism in Africa, the USA refused to buy Cuba's biggest export, cigars. The newsreel featured a short interview with Winston Churchill. In his usual satirical manner, Churchill commented, as he smiled and puffed on his hand-rolled Havana, "The world requires a balance of terror."

In conclusion, the newsreel that afternoon depicted Louie Armstrong, "Satchmo and his Orchestra," embarking on an African peace mission as honorary ambassadors of the US State Department in a vaunted attempt to calm the violence swelling in Katanga. A friendly show of music, but to those involved in the conflict it seemed pathetic rather than diplomatic. Both British and American governments were panicking, fearing communism would influence Africa, strategically affording the Soviets an opportunity of locating long-range nuclear missiles aimed toward Europe.

That evening, Victor had the thought of sending Samuel a letter. He decided to forward a note via airmail, to which, three weeks later, Samuel responded with an air telegram. The telegram offered a telephone number of a secure line where, at certain times of the day, they could talk openly. In 1962, a telephone call to Africa cost a small fortune, so Victor borrowed £5 from his mother and paid Big John a visit to use his business telephone in the saloon bar of the Atlantic pub in Loughborough Junction. Big John was a well-known local villain who had all the latest radios and televisions so he could keep one step ahead.

After a series of operators had finished connecting a line across Europe to the African continent, a multi-national electronic chain was established and a telephone bell rang somewhere in the deepest African Congo.

Victor knew how to assist Samuel before being asked. Their relationship was defined by a commonality of violence and nowhere was more suitable for this than in a war zone. After a short hello, they cut to the chase. Samuel asked for arms to be smuggled into a port somewhere off the Ivory Coast, then transported deep into the Congo where he would take delivery. During Victor's brief but intense conversation, Samuel promised him wealth beyond his wildest dreams. Victor knew Seatankers Inc, and that the *S.S. William R. Folbert* sailed to Africa from Cuba on a regular basis. He also knew that it flew the Panamanian flag, the flag of convenience for shipments that would otherwise be thought illegal.

Samuel was pleased with Victor and said, "Look, my friend... I have many, many more diamonds just like the one I gave you when I was in London. I'll give you anything you want, just tell me what it is you want most. All these things you see before you in your dreams, all those things will be yours if you do this one thing for me!"

Samuel didn't need to beg.

The call lasted seven minutes fifteen seconds but it seemed like hours. On replacing the receiver, Victor became conscious that several people were standing within earshot and must have overheard his every word.

"What was all that about then?" Big John enquired.

"Nothing," said Victor.

"What do you mean, 'nothing'? That didn't sound like nothing to me, did it to you, Jimmy?" John said, turning to one of his sidekicks.

Jimmy struggled for the right thing to say because if it didn't sound like nothing, then how could it sound like anything?

The thought crossed Victor's mind that Big John could be useful after all. He seemed loaded and was always looking for different ways to launder his dirty money. So he decided to tell him something – everything, in fact.

"Only trouble is," said Victor, "it means I have to go to the Congo, just to keep an eye on things and meet my colleague Samuel again."

John didn't need convincing. "Well, count me in, Victor! I like this one! But remember, if you ever cross me, I'll tear you limb from fucking limb!!!"

A cold shiver ran down Victor's spine. He could see John was enjoying this thought. He reassured himself in his usual delusional way by thinking nothing could possibly go wrong. What he didn't know was that Interpol had tapped Samuel's secure line and his call was eavesdropped by the authorities.

Three months later, Victor boarded a steamer once again and set sail for Africa with a copy of *Gray's Anatomy* under his arm, together with forged qualifications, documents that would allow him to pass as a surgeon. Thinking that the arms shipment he had organised weeks earlier was en route to Katanga from Cuba, he relaxed onboard as the ship sailed first into Atlantic waters, then on to African oceans where whales and dolphins swam alongside. He dreamt of his newfound wealth and how rich he was and laughed at the idiots back in England who worked hard for a living. This was the life!

He finally arrived at Port Stanley, only to enter a bloodbath of systematic slaughter, genocide and tribal cleansing fuelled by cocaine. He witnessed bombing, machine-gunning and looting by the NATO-backed government tribal forces. It was horrific. So desperate was the campaign to stop the communists that civilian targets included hospitals, ambulances, churches and schools. Reports of cannibalism and the massacre of missionaries and other civilians were rife, spreading fear among the mass transit of displaced people. Wherever these Congolese troops passed, they left terror, anarchy and chaos. Victor's delusion was overshadowed by bloodshed and death. He would later tell of how he found the tailor's needle and thread, brought with him to darn his socks, perfect for sewing together the flesh of the maimed and dying, his fictitious skills finally being called to task.

Many men, fuelled by morphine looted from Red Cross relief packs, took on legendary powers as they challenged guns with a machete; even after being struck by multiple bullets, they reached the front lines of defence to slaughter the foreign troops. The list of countries becoming embroiled in the mess was getting longer by the day. Mining interests were great, due to the area's rich mineral deposits, diamonds and other precious minerals. The Belgian troops slowly withdrew as Cuban officers commanding the Katangese army pushed forward. Cuba was sympathetic to its Katangese comrades and, in a publicity stunt, Fidel Castro sent troops to Africa to put on a show of support in defiance of the United Nations. The troops he sent were rounded up from volunteer peasant solders loyal to the Castro cause; he christened them "The Internationalists."

Under Samuel's command, these mercenaries were assigned

to a mechanized infantry company equipped with Soviet vehicles to help launch a counter-attack. Instead, it became embroiled in the UN battle of Elizabethville and many were slaughtered within forty-eight hours of arrival. Despite conflicting justifications, the Cuban intervention played well to domestic audiences in Cuba. Fidel's stature improved internationally as he attempted to re-establish himself as the philosophical and martial leader of revolutionary movements throughout the Third World, but at the cost of over a thousand men, his "Internationalists."

The Africans, conditioned by centuries of hatred of the Portuguese slave trade, were initially hostile to the Hispanic Cubans, especially in Cabinda where the foreign arrivals were reported on the primitive telegraphy of drums – beats that could be heard within a radius of some 35 kilometres, describing tortures for the white devils and the elephant traps which lay in wait for them.

Two weeks after Victor's arrival, Samuel learnt of the botched arms shipment and sent a young woman to him with a message of warning. Her long, slender figure moved gracefully through the long African grass as if hovering on water. She could have been mistaken as an Ethiopian, or even a Somalian, were it not for the instantly recognisable scarred cheeks of Katangese ritual marking. She had once been a very beautiful woman who had turned many admiring eyes, but the war had broken her heart. The death she had witnessed had taken away her youth. Although only in her late twenties, her body was already sagging from years of hard work. Her legs, however, were strong and muscular, clear of any of the varicose veins that her contemporary western counterparts may have suffered.

"Victor," she said, "you are a jinx to us, the sorcerer told us so."

"But why? I did everything that General Samuel asked of me! Take me to him, and please let me explain. It wasn't my fault."

The messenger looked at him and said, "Don't you understand, you white fool? If General Samuel sees you again, he will kill you with his bare hands and add your skull to all the other human skulls that he collects. You are bad luck for him. You are a jinx. The only reason you are alive now is because of the kindness you showed him in your country. It is your fault the guns never reached us. It is your fault that your white government robbed us of our freedom. It is all your fault and you deserve to die like the rest of us will today."

Victor was stunned. How had his plan gone so terribly wrong? And for a moment he experienced an emotional disembodiment where everything seemed in the process of disintegration.

At dawn the following morning, flashes of light from shelling radiated on the horizon. Thunderous aftershocks dislodged a million tiny creatures from their gentle footholds high up in the forest canopy, making them plummet to the jungle floor. A living rain of tiny life. The United Nations advanced toward the dense mist and the stillness of jungle air fused with the smell of gasoline and blood in a rich cocktail of 20th century intoxication. The sound of European voices could be heard screaming in distress from deep inside the jungle, sending a cold message along the United Nations line... then stillness as the UN helicopters dropped propaganda leaflets, eager to deploy them and escape the torrent of Russian-made anti-aircraft shells. From the pilot's viewpoint, it was a miniature board game being played out by a thousand toys, rather than a nation of displaced populations seeking identity.

Through the morning mist of burning sunrise, Victor saw the outline of a man wielding a machete in one hand, whilst the other held what looked like a large coconut dangling from its coir, difficult to identify at first but, as the figure drew close, Samuel's eyes were unmistakable. His black skin was now sapphire with congealed blood, the coconut recognisable now as a decapitated head dangling from strands of hair. Like a giant toad diving into the depths of a muddy pond, he moved slowly through the mist; then the apparition dissolved, and for the first time Victor experienced a feeling of infinite desolation. Flying just metres above the trees, a roar of French Mirage jets loosened heavy jackfruits from the upper branches, turning them into organic projectiles that fell brutally to further mutilate the wounded below. The silence shattered, Samuel vanished.

The UN troops sent to terminate African communism had succeeded. Ground troops involved in this infamous action originated from Ireland, Sweden, Italy, Ethiopia and India. Many eyewitnesses, notably the forty-six genuine civilian doctors of Elizabethville, denounced the actions of the UN troops in what was called, "a brutal military campaign." The snuffing out of Katanga's freedom was accompanied by a barbarity seldom witnessed. Victor was detained, questioned and sent for trial as a mercenary. The death penalty was mandatory for mercenaries and in the Katangese capital of Elizabethville, large, heavy, wooden gallows were already being erected in preparation. But, after some months of solitary confinement, much publicity from the Western press and petitioning from the British Consul, Victor was granted a reprieve and extradited to the United Kingdom for sentencing. The "African Trust Service" bank account set up by Big John in London had been frozen, together with his £500,000 investment and Samuel's deposit of 1,000,000 Belgian francs, and the arms shipment from Cuba had been detoured by the Royal Navy to the then Western-friendly coast of Libya, a country Britain was then united with in its fight against communism.

A photograph taken of Victor on death row was published in the *Daily Express*, headlined: **FAKE DOCTOR GOES TO GAOL.** Victor had lost all. It shows him behind bars giving a thumbs up, waving his letter of reprieve while other, less fortunate, souls look on. This compelling photograph portrays Victor as victim, as captive, a white man in black captivity, without telling the true story. The photograph depicts someone he had invented. The photograph went on to be published in magazines both nationally and internationally, including *Paris Match,* together with other staged images of menacing tribal warlords. Text captions went along the lines of: *African cannibals dressed in tribal clothing waving communist-made Kalashnikov machine guns – the revolutionaries' weapon of war.* Under closer scrutiny, however, one can see that this tribal clothing is being worn over cleanly pressed white shirts and hunting shorts purchased from Fortnum & Mason. Far from being the savage warlords portrayed in the press, these were educated men posing for Western photographers in a propaganda game of political strategy, rather than the true artefact. Many of the African tribal chiefs were educated at Eton, many attending the Royal Military Academy at Sandhurst before returning to Africa with imperialist views, including the then unknown dictator Idi Amin, who went on to become military leader and President of Uganda from 1971 to 1979 and who, during his years in power, was backed by Libya's Muammar al-Gaddafi, as well as the Soviet Union and East Germany.

After his deportation from Africa the military police passed Victor to the civil authorities. The judge sentenced him to three years' imprisonment for fraud and impersonating a doctor, and once again sent him to HMP Ford. During this time, Victor co-operated with the prison services in return for a reduced sentence. He told Detective Cunningham everything – details of Big John's involvement, Samuel's plan for gun-running and the money-laundering scam, everything. His list of underworld contacts read like the *Who's Who* of Brixton, all in return for clemency.

Before his release, however, something unforeseen and completely inexplicable happened. He was told by MI5 to share a cell with the then recently captured spy, Guy Burgess, who had been intercepted on his return from Cuba. His introduction to Burgess seems credible, for the African escapade would be seen as furthering the communist cause, not for financial gain. Burgess would have read in the press, known and understood the Russian involvement in Katanga because of the Cuban dependence on Soviet military and financial aid, and the logistical assistance that had became known as "Operation Carlotta." No Cuban initiative operated in Africa without the Kremlin's approval. Without Soviet military hardware, supplies, aircraft, transport ships, and vast sums of hard currency pumped into the Cuban economy, there would have been few, if any, Cuban troops in Africa. Recent declassified documents on display at the Kew National Archive show that Burgess' old Etonian friend, Prime Minister Harold Macmillan, deliberately misled Burgess with regard to his legal status in Britain. When Burgess asked a visiting English delegation to the Soviet Union for permission to sneak into the country and visit his dying mother in Britain on a return trip from Cuba in 1963, Macmillan secretly endorsed his old friend's visit, only to double-cross him and have him arrested on arrival into the country. As it turned out, Burgess snubbed my father without saying a word… clever chap!

This bizarre encounter with MI5 and Burgess complicated matters. Victor's imagination led him to take on the role of a spy character. In effect, he became the spy Ian Fleming forgot to introduce to Bond. Victor's imagination took flight when he listened to John Barry's soundtrack to the film, *From Russia With Love*, sung by Matt Munroe. The LP played late into the night on his Bush mono record player in the corner of his study. It was a set piece to a trite comedy, tapping out fake documents on his Remington typewriter, drifting in and out of fantasy.

My memory of him returning home in a police squad car still seems exciting. He was tanned from the African sun and looking every bit the returning hero. Two reporters from Express Newspapers were outside our house, poised to make shorthand notes in their tiny notebooks as he arrived. They interviewed him, and he vainly posed for photographs next to a scientific microscope; a prop he had bought to provide the plausible air of being a qualified doctor.

Several weeks later, I can remember being interviewed by someone from Social Services, who questioned me about my parents: whether or not I was happy, was my home nice, did I love my parents and did they love me? My answer was always, "Yes!" I somehow knew I would be removed from South Croxted should I hesitate, for it seemed that the danger of the unknown, a life away from South Croxted, was far more daunting than the unhappiness I was familiar with, so of course I lied.

*

It was during Victor's absences that I was able to fully explore South Croxted. One room in particular was always kept locked. I watched him place the key in a biscuit tin, decorated with peaceful English pastoral scenes by Gainsborough, and hide it toward the back of the pantry between the tins of dog food and baked beans. I went to the tin, took out the key and unlocked the door. His writing desk occupied the centre of the room together with a Remington typewriter and a large crystal bowl full of brightly coloured plastic oranges, carefully displayed like a Dutch painting. I opened closed drawers and found a silk bag of gold coins, sovereigns, banknotes and a panoply of military medals. A lower compartment was lined with vivid pornographic photographs in a brown paper bag with the words, *Maurice's Emporium of Magazines Sold & Exchanged,* stamped on its side. By the look of the dog-eared contents, the magazines had been thumbed by countless other men. Perhaps that was part of their attraction, an unspoken taboo. There was a heavy Victorian photograph album that concealed a musical box in its base that played *Greensleeves,* but the book itself was totally devoid of photographs – no memories. However, all else faded into insignificance at the delight of the bottom drawer, where I found a loaded revolver. All these things, documents, gold, explicit descriptions of sexual organs in activity, held no value by comparison.

I picked up the revolver from its resting place. To hold a real gun was magical. I was now the leading man in my favourite television programme, *I Spy,* an espionage TV drama with a sense of humour staring black actor Bill Cosby. I thought Cosby was the coolest thing I had ever seen, and he was. The gunshots in the theme music really did it for me. The fusion of secret agents posing as top-seeded tennis players in exotic Hong Kong, just gave it that sexy edge.

I tucked the gun into the front pocket of my shorts, but its colossal weight pulled them down below my waist. I tried to raise the pistol with both hands, but it made my small seven-year-old arms ached as I struggled to keep them upright. What kind of metal made this so heavy? Certainly not the type used to make my toy guns. I looked down its barrel and counted the bullets, five shiny rounds glistening inside their dark chambers; the sixth was presumably loaded into its barrel. Its smell reminded me of spent fireworks. I carefully placed the revolver back into the drawer, making sure its position was exactly as I had found it, closed the cupboard and turned the key to lock the door. I would return to the revolver on a later occasion to find three of the once-full chambers emptied. The gun had been fired.

I imagined myself using the gun later in life, when I became the centre of a teenage vendetta at a Crystal Palace May Day fairground. It involved a local hoodlum, Eddy Watts. Although Eddy was in his early twenties, he was a retard with the mentality of a five-year-old. It was cool to hang with Eddy. Nothing could touch you if you were with Eddy because everyone was scared of him. That afternoon, we walked from West Norwood to a run-down branch of Woolworths. I didn't know it at the time, but Eddy was light-fingered and was already known to the local security guards for shoplifting. Then *bingo!*, before I knew it Eddie was making a run for the door with a bottle of Brut Fabergé aftershave hanging from his jacket pocket.

He turned to me and threw the contraband toward me and I had no option but to catch it. As I did so, some middle-aged overweight hero from security tackled me to the ground. Meanwhile, Eddy escaped, leaving me to do the explaining. Later that day, I learnt of his arrest and that he had accused me of being the mastermind behind the plot. Eddy was put away for six convictions of burglary and wouldn't be back in the neighbourhood for two years. Two years was good, because I wouldn't be in the neighbourhood in two years.

Dangle 1963

Along the Thames for six miles and to a depth of three inland, London groaned and festered in a heady mixture of 1960s optimism and post-war depression. On an ordnance survey map it was simply a boundary between the city and its adjoining neighbours, but in the psyche of Big John it was his quarry, a living creature that needed milking. Big John elicited riches from prostitution and illegal immigrants, extorting protection funds from adult pursuits such as Maurice's blue movie cinema, bookies, dog-fighting dens and risqué pubs including The Bricklayers Arms. His language was muscle and it communicated effectively what he wanted most in life: money. Now his mind focused on Victor, or to be more precise, vanquishing the wrong he felt Victor had inflicted on him. John enjoyed violence. He had no empathy for his victims. He knew the memory of old sins could be destroyed by the madness of new ones and thought evil, sickening thoughts. He was an angry child trapped inside the shape of a frightening man.

"I'll not be done over by anyone, especially by a fucking nigger. Fuck Victor and fuck the coon. If he thinks this is *The Black 'n' White-fucking-Minstrel Show,* he got another think coming."

The gait of his walk was small, like a child's, forcing his huge mass to lean forward ever so slightly, as if being pushed by a strong wind. He was straight-backed, as if a length of iron ran the length of his spine. It was the look of a man in need of a crap.

Prison had immured John from a society that took life itself, for the death sentence was still judicial. Convicted murderers in Britain were hung by the neck until dead, courtesy of Britain's last hangman, Harry Allen, who kept an execution diary, a matter-of-fact execution journal to record the details of each condemned prisoner's age, weight, height and final words. Before the execution, he made a point of shaking the prisoner's hand, not in friendship, but to calculate the body's weight and position the height of the rope's knot. His notes also included calculations on the length of rope and drop, and how long prisoners would take to die, usually between nine and eleven seconds, the heaver the quicker. Allen was known for his flamboyant neckties that he famously wore when carrying out his grim trade. Yorkshire-born, he ran pubs in Farnsworth and Whitefield, and performed twenty-nine executions and assisted in fifty-three others between 1938 and 1964.

His last job as Britain's chief executioner was the hanging of murderer Gwynne Owen Evans at HMP Strangeways in Manchester, at 8am on 13 August 1964. She was one of the final two executed in Britain, with the hangings carried out simultaneously. The job had its perks as one could sell inch-sized pieces of used rope to those who thought it held "curative powers," for example, as a cure for migraines. To others, however, it was simply used as a horrific memento. Although John was not yet on the Allen ledger, he was surely moving in that direction. "I'm off to see Allen," became the long-running family joke every time Victor left the house.

The face of Big John was cursed with a cruel appearance, the look of a man struggling in a winter's storm, the look of the lost seeking direction. No rules were Big John's rules... everything he touched, he wanted and eventually owned. He was the king of the underworld and the underworld was the *News of the World!* The thought of the Africans lording it up on the money he had squirreled away for his retirement bolthole in Spain's Costa del Sol was intolerable to him. Big John was convinced he had been done over by one of the oldest tricks in the book, that Victor had taken him on a "419" ride. 419 was a fraud named after the relevant section of the Nigerian Criminal Code, popular in West African organised criminal networks and resulting in a massive proliferation of such confidence tricks from that country. 419 involved a myriad of scams – mail and telephone promises designed to facilitate victims parting with money, involving requests to help move large sums of money, with the promise of a substantial share of the cash in return. The thought of this was becoming too much for John; his biological mixture of adrenalin and testosterone would explode with considerable force. It needed an outlet...

One evening, John invited Maurice, the proprietor of

Maurice's Emporium of Magazines Sold & Exchanged, to a private screening of a movie he had championed, titled *Never Better*. The screening took place in John's hideaway, Sam's Junk Shop in Brixton. John had sponsored Maurice to produce and direct the film, and paid the actors handsomely to make its masochism as authentic as possible. After the screening, everyone left apart from Maurice, who was asked to stay a little longer in order to discuss some unfinished business.

"Now Maurice, you and I are going to play a little game," said John.

He walked over to a 16mm movie camera placed on a tripod and started filming, pointing it towards the chair on which Maurice sat.

"What kind of game, John?"

"What kind of game, Maurice?" John repeated. "You'll see... I want you to put this on."

John threw him a black rubber head mask, the sort used as a bondage fetish. "And take your shirt off, too!"

John then slipped a single nylon stocking over his own head, blurring his features and pulled a pair of pink marigold washing gloves over his outsized hands. Moving to the record player, he put on some music. It was *Shakin' All Over*, a rock and roll song performed by Johnny Kidd and the Pirates.

"Nothing like a good soundtrack," he said, smiling. "Now, sit down and put these on."

He threw Maurice a brown paper bag. Inside it were two pairs of handcuffs. "Put one pair on your ankles and the other on your wrists," he ordered.

Maurice did as John said, then started to cry; he knew what was about to happen.

"You call that a fucking snuff movie?" John taunted.

Maurice nodded his head.

"Well then, tell me something you little cunt. Why did I see that fucking bitch walking through Soho yesterday? When I say I want a snuff movie, I want the fucking real thing."

John's mind fixed on Maurice to release his frustration.

"Please, John, I'm scared! Please release me, let me go."

"Let you go? Who do you think you are? Engelbert Humperdinck?"

John had already planned his entertainment for Maurice and lifted a black holdall onto a tabletop. Maurice's chair stood by a large circular manhole to a Victorian sewer, a hole that fell thirty feet into the effluents of Brixton.

John turned around, holding a hangman's noose. "This, er, rope is the very same rope used to drop Bentley," he said. "I know because I bought it directly from Allen in Wandsworth prison, and that very same rope is going to offer you a way out of your predicament."

He then threw the rope over a ceiling rafter and placed its noose over Maurice's head.

"Stand!" John ordered.

"But I can't stand! Please, John!"

John pulled Maurice to his feet, pulling the rope tight. He lifted the rubber mask and forced a child's softball into Maurice's mouth to stop him screaming. Pulling the rope even tighter, he forced Maurice to stand on tiptoe, teetering on the edge of the chair. Opening the black holdall again, he took out a bloodied electric drill with a drill bit already attached, the sort used to drill thin holes into soft wood so it wouldn't crack when bigger screws were forced into position.

Maurice defecated and he began blacking out. He knew this was John's trademark torture instrument. His legs could no longer support his small, overweight body and as his head became light from hyperventilating, he slumped forward. Slowly, the process of asphyxiation began, just as John had planned.

"Now, that's what I call a snuff movie! No one can accuse me of being wrong, because you would rather die than take pain, wouldn't you?"

Maurice's fat body shook as his nervous system started to close down, trembling like a fish on the end of a hook. At the very last moments of Maurice's life, John released the rope and Maurice fell to the floor in a wobbling splat. Removing the rubber mask, John opened Maurice's eyes as he spat out the ball, gasping for breath.

"Get my point?" John said with a smile.

"Yes, I totally understand, John."

Unlocking the handcuffs, John gathered his valuable rope together and placed it back into its holdall.

"Now, fuck off back to Victoria and have a bath. You stink of shit."

"Yes, John, I will, John."

And with that, Maurice dressed and stumbled from the house, making sure that he wasn't being followed and ran straight to the police. He knew that whatever crimes or depravities he had committed in the past, nothing could be as horrific as the punishment John could inflict on him. There was no way he could ever make a real snuff movie, not for all the money in Brixton.

Victor was next on John's list. Shadows were beginning to gather for the Richardsons.

★

For many years, my mother Stella was forced to fend alone and provide for her family. She found work as a barmaid in a Courage pub, The Bricklayers Arms, and was welcomed by the governor, a Mr. Stanley Jolly, the proprietor. Jolly's ruddy complexion exposed an alcoholic occupation. Snow-white hair and a yellow moustache that thatched his upper lip, burnt umber yellow from the unfiltered cigarettes perpetually balanced on his lower lip. Jolly took pity on my mother. He had spent long enough behind the counters of public houses to read people and understand their worries. A good landlord is a good listener and how he listened to my mother! In Victor's absence, Jolly introduced her to a number of gentlemen admirers from the bar, where metal tankards hung above the great French-polished counter and glass-engraved fake Gothic splendour. She was on her way up in the world and one evening she was introduced to Bob, or, to be more precise, Detective Inspector Robert Cunningham from Scotland Yard's newly formed Special Branch, the "Specials."

Although only in his late forties, Cunningham was already old for his years. He had killed many men in Italy while fighting the Nazis and had seen more death than many. DI Cunningham had a gruff voice brought on from drinking neat Johnny Walker and smoking unfiltered Senior Service cigarettes. His catch phrase was, "Wait a minute… doesn't that mean…?" One evening he gave her a gift, a Kodak Instamatic camera. She asked him:

"What's this?"

"It's for you," he said. "Will you keep me informed?"

"About?"

"Victor. Anything that concerns you about his behaviour. Anything you think might affect your family."

"Why would you want to help me?" she said.

"Because the police have a duty, and, more importantly, I like you!"

Cunningham, with his brightest of crystal blue eyes, played the ageing Errol Flynn look-alike who fell deeply, madly, in love with my mother. He was solicitous from the first time their eyes met. He had decided to take a non-uniform role after becoming embroiled in large-scale deployments of police officers to stop sit-down demonstrations in support of the Campaign for Nuclear Disarmament, or CND. That was enough for him. Large-scale civil unrest didn't fit his vocation, he was old school. I often found his tweed jacket resting over the banisters in our house, together with the lingering smell of malt whisky. Later in life I asked my mother about him and she freely admitted that he dearly loved her.

"He once asked me to run away with him… but how could I when I was responsible for you? He could have shown you a path less complicated in this world, one that would have guided you. I always promised myself that I would not love you the way

Victor's mother loved him. I saw her love corrupt him and swore it would never happen to you. He came close to destroying me because of her, and I will not allow you to destroy another woman in the same way it almost destroyed me."

Cunningham had an assistant, Sergeant Sean Casey, an Irishman. He was the silent partner. He dressed way above the salary of a copper and listened intently, paying particular attention to conversations about my father. Priests in a Catholic grammar school just outside Belfast had educated Casey. Church was essential every weekend, when he had a chance to purge his sins at confession. He had a particular interest in Victor's activities because Victor kept company with criminals. Gaining information about the underworld through my mother was a method that went against police procedure. But that didn't stop Casey from planning, and Cunningham from falling in love with her. Despite his tender age of twenty-three, Casey had risen to the dizzying heights of sergeant, placing him head and shoulders above the other bastards in Special Branch. With straight "A"s from Hendon Police Training College, he had a chip on his shoulder, with a lot to prove in a world he saw as the devil's playground. He was keen to move to "London Central" but secretly hated the British for the way the Irish were always the butt end of the joke, in the same class as the immigrants from the West Indies. Cunningham and Casey were working on four cases at the same time. That was a lot of legwork, a lot of paper, meaning a lot of unfinished typing. Far better to lose it, or turn a blind eye to the odd incident... there was more to be gained by drinking and listening.

Listening was something Victor never did. Despite being encouraged to learn how to drive, both by his mother and Stella, he had no interest. In his usual self-centred way he thought what good was a car to a seafaring man, a sailor on dry land? So it was with great interest that he discovered that Jimmy drove an Amphicar Backgrounder, a car-boat because it could be driven both on roads and on water, even the sea, powered by a propeller at its rear that could be engaged by the manual gear. It was the perfect getaway car. The Amphicar was manufactured in Berlin, Germany from 1962 to 1967, the only non-military amphibious vehicle ever put into production on a commercial basis. The many rules and regulations for road and water going vehicles make it very unlikely that another car-based amphibian will ever be produced again.

The Amphicar appealed to my imagination – a car that's a boat, great! One Sunday, Jimmy took me out for a drive to Kent. We passed farms with their strange looking oast-houses and hop fields he worked as a child with his Cockney family, to pick hops for beer-making, We ventured across small rivers when the wheels stopped and the propeller shaft came into action, and drove across open fields, startling herds of cows and levelling one or two fences in the process. Our destination was the place he was raised, the Young Offender's Institute. As its great gates opened, we drove onto the forecourt of a grand Victorian home. A grey-haired, elderly, taciturn gent with no facial emotion greeted me with a stern gaze. His well-furrowed face and piercing blue eyes matched his hand-knitted blue woollen turtleneck, that seemed an odd choice of clothing since it was such a punishingly hot day.

We drove back to South Croxted through the hop fields of Kent. That late afternoon we watched *Sunday Night at the London Palladium* on television. Headlining were a troupe of magicians dressed in dramatic traditional Chinese robes, baggy sleeves and long, pencil-like moustaches. Of course, many of the illusions so eagerly observed were based in science; combustible gunpowder, refractive optics, precise measurements, unlike Jimmy, who promoted a science of another kind.

During Jimmy's time in prison, he had shared a cell with a pigeon fancier and had decided to start racing our feathered friends. He'd seen the film, *The Birdman of Alcatraz* and was convinced it was for him. Jimmy found a freedom in watching them fly that he had never experienced before. It was his link to some sort of therapeutic reality, a reality portrayed by honest working men from the North where the sport of racing pigeons began, no doubt due to their confinement underground digging for coal. Pigeon fancying was the sport of working men, filed somewhere between dog racing and cock fighting.

Jimmy's menagerie grew larger. Next came rat breeding, followed by dog breeding, miniature ponies and parrots, all squeezed together in a space of fifteen square meters, cramped indeed. Then Jimmy lost interest and slowly the animals began to suffer. One by one they died, either through neglect or ill health, until a neighbour reported it to the RSPCA and the remaining creatures were removed. One of Jimmy's last acquisitions was a pedigree German Shepherd named *Tiger*, who I adopted. Although I was never told I could keep him, he was mine and he was alive and loved.

As time passed, I became overshadowed by Jimmy's bipolar disorder and, to avoid his schizophrenic ventures, went wherever he was not. He continued offending throughout my childhood. On a number of occasions, I accompanied my sister on visits to see him in prison, especially Parkhurst. The prison was first built as a military hospital in 1805 and was later transformed to a prison for boys awaiting deportation, mainly to Australia. My sister and I would start our journey from Victoria Railway Station to Spithead in Portsmouth. Then came the mainland crossing of the Solent Channel to the Isle of Wight from Ryde, by hovercraft, and that's where my absolute fascination for science blossomed. How marvellously futuristic an invention the hovercraft is, and so speedy! A hovercraft, or air-cushion vehicle (ACV), is a craft designed to travel over any smooth surface supported by a cushion of slow-moving, high-pressure air, ejected downwards against the surface below, and contained within a "skirt." I liked the hovercraft, a strange way of travelling in my father's saltwater footsteps without touching the sea. It was always the sea, the thought of the sea and its vast, undulating dark depths that held a mystery, a calling.

Vermilion Moon

THE CRESCENT OF THE MOON appeared blood red from earth-shine. It made the South London night feel as if it belonged to another world. This celestial abnormality bought out the lunatic fraternity warning of the "End of The World," but the Astronomer Royal explained the phenomenon on the BBC evening news.

"The red appearance of the moon is caused by *Rayleigh Scattering*," he said. "Very tiny particles in the atmosphere are deflecting light in random directions inversely proportional to the wavelength to the fourth power. Warm air currents cause this optical phenomenon, carried from Africa due to abnormal weather conditions across the subcontinent, and this ill wind is loosening a fine dust high above the London sky in the form of a dust storm. For those who think this is the end of the world, let me assure you, you are completely deluded."

If only the Astronomer Royal had lived at South Croxted, he may have given credence to lunatic prophecy when the loathsome figure of Big John appeared at the door to rectify his loss and continue his own style of scientific brutality.

At eleven o'clock, the Brixton Town Hall clock chimed ten. The sound of John and his thugs forcing open our front door muffled the eleventh. Its latch, old and worn, buckled, snapped and sprang open falling to the ground like a hairpin shaken loose by the toss of a young girl's hair.

"Where's the cunt you call a father?" demanded John, his breath tarred with tobacco and smelling of brandy sweat. His teeth were crooked and brown as if rinsed in excrement. His long, dark sideburns covered scarred, pockmarked cheeks, forming a pincer movement across the top of his thin lips. His complexion was pallid marble in contrast to his flamingo-pink bald scalp. He wanted to kill, needed to hurt, to reinstate his authority. His huge feet matched his huge neck that balanced his monster head. He was an object of colossal form, a great mass which radiated gravity, attracting smaller bodies that became trapped in his orbit. Virtual clones, like little replica freaks, to one day become big freaks that would colonise this tiny corner of South London where the first fascist traits of the British Nationalist Party were in the making. This was the event horizon, a black hole generating dark power that the Astronomer Royal would not find in any textbook.

"But we're not allowed to call him that," I said. I didn't know the meaning of the word "cunt," but made sure to remember it for future use.

Thinking I was mocking him, one of the younger thugs said, "Shut your little fucking gowb and tell us where he is."

This hoodlum was dressed in a dark blue crushed velvet suit with a white-laced front shirt. He looked like a pop star, very à la mode. The contrast of violence, idiocy and fashion consumed me with curiosity.

"Come on, Jimmy, he's only a kid. For fuck's sake leave him," said another.

Jimmy. So that's your name, I thought.

Then pandemonium broke out as the thugs went about their work with the eager delight of a child let loose in Disneyland. They took to their drudgery, smashing everything and anything of value; they turned on my fourteen-year-old brother, Raymond, punching his face until his lips dripped blood. I started repeating the Lord's Prayer over and over again, waiting for Jesus to miraculously appear in a blinding light to protect us, but he didn't. The house was ransacked and Grandmother and I were pushed into the tiny back room scullery, where she pissed herself and began shaking violently as she fell into the cold, unlit, fireplace.

John produced a sawn-off shotgun from under his long overcoat and screamed, "Tell your fucking father he's a dead man. When I find him, I'll fucking kill him. Say Big John was 'ere, right?"

"Big John was 'ere," I repeated, nodding like an obedient toy dog.

With that, the pricks left, taking with them a volatile mixture of testicular force and psychopathic paranoia. Henrietta, my grandmother, lay on her side in the corner of the cold fireplace, sobbing, face wet with tears. This eighty-two-year-old woman had been reduced to a scared, trembling wreck, from which she never recovered.

At twelve o'clock Victor returned. I could hear his Chelsea boots crunching on glass as he went through the house without so much as a word. He unlocked the splintered cabinet that was overturned on the floor and removed the revolver from its hiding place. His face fixed and expressionless, he was in a trance, his eyes focused beyond their surroundings. He then straddled my brother's wheel buckled bicycle and cycled toward Brixton and darkness, making a swishing sound, like a mad delicatessen slicing the pitch of night.

A Mark II Zephyr was parked across the road. Its constabulary blue light was stowed in the glove compartment for now, as Detective Inspector Cunningham and Sergeant Casey savoured the chase about to ensue. Turning the engine on, they drove slowly away, tailing Victor to John's hideout. They were about to make the arrest of their careers...

One could have located John's hideout by a bitter smell of fire damage compressed with a stink radiating from an open sewer in the yard attached to the property. Such was the vile odour that during the summer, dogs would scratch the door to the enclosure in search of rotting food. God only knows what foul things happened in that terrible place. But one can assume that much incriminating evidence was disposed of through that manhole in the backyard after burning.

It was a tumbledown wreck of a house, its loose brickwork home to wild weeds growing from every gap. Broken, half-boarded windows were painted black from the inside. The house represented all that was evil in Brixton, with its sprawling open yard, a home to vermin, and the gut-wrenching smell of human decay that swallowed the darkness. The sound of a woman's screams could be heard coming from the upstairs; John was busy filming some poor destitute soul, perhaps another rehearsal following that of Maurice.

Victor shouted to a faintly illuminated upstairs window, to the room where the activity seemed to be taking place. "Why do you want to kill me John? It wasn't my fault!"

Untangling himself from a cocoon of sweaty soiled sheets, John opened the window to look at Victor on the pavement below. Cunningham arrived and got out of the car. He assessed the situation unfolding on the other side of the road and second-guessed what was about to happen.

The hairs on the back of Victor's neck stood up as he realised that John was pointing a shotgun toward him. Cunningham pulled back his shoulders, tightened his buttocks and walked toward Victor who had frozen in confusion; his pupils widened as the two men locked eyes.

"He's got previous, you know," Cunningham said.

"Who the fuck are you?" said John, now pointing the gun at Cunningham. "What do you mean, 'previous'?"

"Oh, one or two attacks, altercations. You see, if there's one thing a copper hates most, it's being called out to a domestic. After all, that's what this is. Isn't it, John? A domestic?"

"Yer… that's right, a domestic, so piss off."

"The problem is, John, that domestics always end unsatisfactorily. But this one's different, at least its outcome will be. I want you to put the gun down because there's more than one police officer in attendance. There's me and then another pointing a revolver at the back of your head as I speak and unless you place your gun down on the floor immediately, I will instruct him to fire."

Victor was confused, emotional. Cunningham's wartime training had kicked in and his anger at being put into this awkward situation outweighed his own sense of survival.

"During the war I killed many a better man than you, John. Were you in the war? No, I forgot. You were too busy shagging nice little West Indian girls."

With that, Big John fired the shotgun, just missing Cunningham's left shoulder. *Nothing puts a man off his aim better than agitating him,* Cunningham thought.

Sergeant Casey entered the room and discharged three well-aimed rounds with the precision of a trained executioner, hitting John's huge fingers and ricocheting from his sovereign rings which could barely fit over his enormous knuckles. John dropped his weapon as a gush of blood fell onto the dirty sheets covering the young woman who was hiding underneath. John had lost his left ear. It was a symphony of noise that sent nesting pigeons fluttering from the broken roof in panic. Dogs awoke from their dreams to bark down empty streets and a scream from the traumatised woman accompanied the ear-ringing explosion of gunshot.

Turning to Victor, Cunningham said, "Fuck off out of my sight, you little prick, before I have you shot, too…"

Victor ran into the night, passing the tramps sitting on the steps of the railway station and the drunks leaving the Atlantic pub, where the sound of their horrible laughter was accompanied by shouts of young men brawling, encouraged by their girls. He leapt over the railings of Brockwell Park and raced back to South Croxted, where he clung to my mother who comforted him as if he were a baby. In her compassion and soothing sounds she hid a secret, for she knew far more about that night's events than she could have said.

*

John's arrest hung over Brixton like an invisible fog. The hush of his absence made everything feel a little lighter than before and Victor, at least for now, was off the hook. In the harsh morning light, the full extent of the damage to our home was apparent. Queues formed at the bus stop opposite our house as people waited to catch the early bus but instead caught a glimpse of the violent aftermath. How they stared. At 8am the hunchbacked dwarf salesman, father of Julian Smalley, the bullied kid in my school class who had inherited his father's condition, called to collect his monthly hire-purchase repayments only to find the front door hanging from its hinges with nowhere to knock. He manoeuvred his dwarf body into the hallway and called to my mother.

"Hello. Everything all right, Mrs Richardson, only your front door seems to have been kicked in?"

"Yes, thank you!" she irritably replied from the front room, as she strained to lift the overturned bookcase to an upright position. He moved forward a few feet.

"Only I would offer to lend a hand but you know, being my size and all, I don't often come across this sort of thing. However, one service that may be of interest to you is our new furniture lease scheme. The repayments are most reasonable and I could negotiate a good deal for you and Mr Richardson, of course."

"No, thank you," she said, gritting her teeth as she finally managed to push the bookcase back up. "I'm sure we can suffice, albeit a little worse for wear!" she added.

"I see. Well then, I'll wish you a good day and best of luck with the household rearrangements." Reading the situation, he thought better than to ask for that month's repayment.

"I'll call again soon then!" And with that, the little chap clumsily made his way back out of the house. Waddling his little body across the splinters of smashed glass without so much as a sound, he put on his trilby hat, and opened the door to his sky blue, three-wheeled Reliant Robin Deluxe to exit. *Some folks do the strangest things,* he thought, as he started the engine and began whistling *These Boots Are Made For Walking,* by Nancy Sinatra.

Friday's edition of The London Evening News, *18th October 1963*

KILLER ARRESTED BY COPS

Following a warrant for the arrest of underworld fugitive John Fowler, police from Scotland Yard Special Branch made a major breakthrough yesterday. An arrest was made outside the Brixton Labour Exchange, Coldharbour Lane, following an armed battle with the police. Fowler, aged 42, is wanted for questioning regarding what is believed to be the abduction and torture of Maurice Arnold earlier this week. Interpol had also previously issued a request for Fowler's arrest for alleged money laundering and illegal gunrunning to the African Congo. A spokesman for the Met Police commented:

"The detention of John Fowler relates to a number of serious incidents which are of the utmost concern to the force. We will see to it that the Maurice Arnold affair is rigorously investigated together with the other associated accusations, consummate with British law, and all culprits are brought to heel!"

Martin aged 1

Parents circa 1955

Victor during World War II, wearing the British Merchant Seamen's uniform that became his amulet against danger the rest of his life.

Victor at sea, circa 1961

Stella and Victor, 1957

Martin, South Croxted Road, 1962

Victor and Martin, 1964

Stella with Martin's grandmother Henrietta, 1962.

Stella pregnant with Martin, with Raymond, Linda and grandmother,
Margate Beach 1958.

Uncle Len and Aunty Margaret drinking a beer.

*Victor and Stella on their wedding day outside
Westminster Registry Office, 1957.*

Print more Feet please

Stella in the garden. Note type: "Print more feet please."
Victor refused to accept the negative was uncropped, 1957.

Seafaring men: Victor together with merchant navy sailors, 1956.

Victor flexing his muscle aboard ship destined for Africa, 1962.

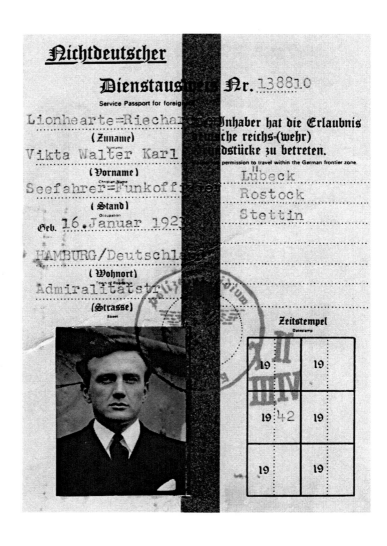

Nichtdeutscher

Dienstausweis Nr. 138810

Service Passport for foreign

Lionhearte=Riechar... Inhaber hat die Erlaubnis
....che reichs-(wehr)
(Zuname) ...dstücke ʒu betreten.

Vikta Walter Karl permission to travel within the German frontier zone.
(Vorname)
Christian Name
                                    Lübeck
Seefahrer=Funkoffizier
.... Rostock
(Stand)
Occupation   Stettin
Geb. 16.Januar 192...

HAMBURG/Deutschla...
(Wohnort)
Town of Residence
Admiralitätstr...
(Strasse)
Street

Zeitstempel
Datestamp

19	19
19 42	19
19	19

Among the forgeries and assumed identities…

Victor, the would-be spy, 1964

Signature of holder ~~_____~~ _[signature]_

Date of Birth _16·1·1923_

Place of Birth _CLAPHAM   LONDON_

DESCRIPTION OF HOLDER :

Height _____5_____ feet ____11____ inches.

Colour of Eyes ____HAZEL____

Colour of Hair ____BROWN____

Complexion ____FRESH____

Any special peculiarities ____—____

Complexion: "Fresh"

'DOCTOR'S' DREAM WORLD CRASHES AGAIN

Express Staff Reporter

ELISABETHVILLE, Tuesday.

WHEN Victor Lione-hearte - Reichardson arrived in Katanga he called himself "Colonel Doctor" and asked for a uniform—with medals.

He took over the medical control of north - east Katanga and ran a big hospital.

But today the dream world of Lionehearte-Reichardson (born William Biddlecombe) crashed —again.

An Elisabethville court gave him a suspended sentence of eight months' jail for forging medical certificates and practising without proper qualifications.

THE 'DOCTOR'
" I tried to be good "

The fact that he could forge certificates well enough to deceive the professor in charge of medical services, that he cautiously evaded trying any surgery, that he asked to be posted out to Baudouinville instead of remaining in the city here, and that he asked for the best possible medical orderlies—all this indicates that he knew very well what he was doing and that he is responsible for his actions.

Headline from the Daily Express, 25th September 1962.
Note caption: The 'Doctor'—"I tried to be good"

81

Victor imprisoned in Katanga by the United Nations, 1962.

Katanga, circa 1963

General Tshombe, Katanga

The fake doctor posing with Gray's Anatomy.

Family poses for press photographers moments after Victor's return home from Africa, 1963.

MARRIAGE OVER, SAYS CONGO PRISONER'S WIFE

Express Staff Reporter

THE wife of Victor Lionehearte-Reichardson heard yesterday that her husband had been released from a Katanga prison and said: "Our marriage is on the rocks."

At their home in South Croxted-road, D u l w i c h, London, she said: "As far as I am concerned the marriage is over unless he returns a very different man.

"But I don't think he will ever change."

Her 39-year-old husband, an ex - dining - car attendant, was jailed for eight months in October for posing as a doctor at a hospital in Katanga after forging medical documents in London

He assisted with several minor operations and was said to have saved some lives.

Last night he was flying back to England.

The news of his sudden release came as a shock to his 33-year-old wife Stella, mother of a daughter of 15 and sons aged 12 and four.

She said: "We have nothing in common any more. He doesn't like football or going out. His real job is a radio officer in the Merchant Navy.

Very happy

"Without him these last few months life has been very happy, and unless he alters a lot that's how I would like it to stay."

She added: "I must admit he has been very good to my youngest boy."

IN ELISABETHVILLE Lionehearte - Reichardson (born William Biddlecombe) said his release order had been signed by President Tshombe.

He looked fit and sunburned and said: "My only aim now is to get out of this country fast."

WIFE STELLA
"He'll never change"

Daily Express story, 1963

Victor posing for a photographer from the Daily Express after his release from the United Nations prison in Africa, 1962.

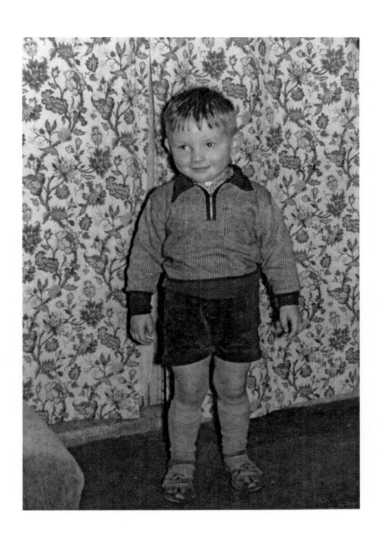

Martin in front of closed curtains to the dark garden.

*Martin's mother cutting out her image from mementos of the past,
Butlin's Holiday Camp, Camber Sands.*

Martin playing in the yard at South Croxted, 1961.

Victor in hot climes, Cuba 1962

Show your girl friends
this photograph of
English beef cake .

Back: "Show your girlfriends this photograph of English beefcake."

The Cat's Whiskers 1965

IT WAS A SATURDAY NIGHT AT THE CAT'S WHISKERS. My sister was dancing the twist with her friend Christine when she saw Jimmy at the bar buying everyone drinks. Jimmy thought himself as a James Cagney, a little Caesar, but Linda saw him for what he was, a shit.

The Cat's Whiskers on Streatham Hill was a very popular place. A purpose-built dance hall in South London, it was part of family history since my mother had met Victor there in 1942, when the hall was called the Locarno. Victor looked handsome in his wartime seaman's uniform and when he asked her to dance with him to the music of Billy Cotton's big brass band, how could she refuse? In her eyes, she saw a good-looking man in uniform, who talked with a studied middle-class accent. He was her *Mr. Wonderful,* the epitome of a well-groomed male, respectable, upstanding, charming and a great actor. She, like many others, had fallen for him. (The dance hall gained a macabre claim to fame in the 1950s, when Ruth Ellis, the last woman to be hanged in Britain, for the murder of her lover David Blakeley in 1955, worked there, serving drinks for the semi-celebs and the Kray Twins.)

That night, Linda knew she was going to say something wrong before even opening her mouth. She was ready for it. She was up for a fight.

"Oh no, Christine, look, it's him!"

"Who, you silly cow?"

"Em, over there, that Jimmy who did my house in. He's giving me a dirty look."

"What? The dirty ------!"

"Flipping heck, he's got a cheek."

"Go on, 'ave a word. I'd go round the bend if I were you."

"You're right, I will."

Linda walked through the throbbing mass of teenagers twisting around the centre of the dance hall, to the corner of the bar where Jimmy held forth. Her painted face and vermilion-coloured lips made her look much older that she was. More sophisticated.

"Curse you! Not so big now, are you?" she said.

"What do you want?" said Jimmy,

"Now your pay-master's banged up!"

"Yer, well, he's a diamond geezer."

"You know what? My granny died because of what you and your diamond geezer did."

"I never heard of her. Are you crazy? How old are you, any-way?"

"I'm nearly sixteen," she said.

"Well, before you take vengeance into your own hands, I want you to dance with me so I can say sorry. Will you?"

Linda looked over at the mass of people on the dance floor, all having fun as the lights dimmed and the music changed to the slower beat of The Four Tops. The deep blue light of the dance hall gave Jimmy an edgy, handsome, attractiveness and she just couldn't help herself.

"Sure, why not?" she said. "You know what, I don't give a shit any more because this is just another piece of shit piled on top of an already high pile of shits, so this shit makes no difference."

"Well, 'ark at you. Little Miss Tough, aren't we?" said Jimmy.

Not much of a conversation, but I suppose for any tender fifteen-year-old girl who despised her father as much as Linda despised Victor, what better way of persecuting him than dancing with his enemy? It was a runic rhyme as two months later, she fell pregnant with Jimmy's child.

My mother understood why Linda had chosen her companion. After all, she had done the same thing to her father, Jack, by choosing Victor. I guess that's something some girls do? It's the ultimate retaliation for being unloved.

Jimmy was a Borstal boy. He had been raised in a young offenders' institution from the age of six, where he learnt how to walk with the cocky swagger of a killer and the punch of a dirty fighter. He was ready for the streets. At sixteen, he was serving time in Wormwood Scrubs, mixing with men twice his age. His image was slick. He based his look on bands like The Four Tops, The Supremes and Smokey Robinson and the Miracles, as he loved anything and everything Detroit. The black sound of Motown complemented his two-tone suits, brogue shoes, white button-down collar Ben Sherman shirts, short-cropped hair and Sta-Press trousers which finished halfway up the leg. Spade music with white fashion. A contradiction of values, style over racism and something very British... the early skinhead. Jimmy was about to serve a stretch in a string of high security prisons including Parkhurst on the Isle of Wight, for attempted armed robbery with grievous bodily harm. It was thought that by moving inmates from prison to prison, it stopped them from forming gangs; it was known as "The Ghost Train."

My sister's wedding day in 1966 was held at Brixton Registry Office. Even though she was five months pregnant, she managed to hide the bump and continue wearing mini-skirts and heels. I was eight when my nephew, Ross, was born. The wedding remains a memory as clear and sharp as the Savile Row suits worn by the small-time gangsters from Brixton. The criminals who assembled outside the registry office, opposite the police station, made for an impressive line-up of some of South London's most wanted. The reception party at our house was even more memorable. Ginny the lesbian worked with my mother, behind the bar. It was a simultaneous wedding celebration and a farewell to the groom. Jimmy was now part of our family.

"Make mine a Champagne!" said Stella, in her best Audrey Hepburn impression.

"More like Babycham!" said Ginny.

They both erupted into hysterical laughter as Ginny pressed her beer-drenched T-shirt against Stella and danced. Her erect nipples were clearly visible as she seized the moment and whispered into Stella's ear, "Why don't you leave him, Stella? You know you could do so much better."

"I know I could, but that's what makes it so much fun!" she replied.

"Leave him then," said Ginny.

Stella thought about it as she looked toward the doorway to see my father sitting on the landing outside the party room alone, drinking lemonade and eating slices of wedding cake away from the other guests. After the Big John incident, Victor took to wearing his uniform like a baby's security blanket despite its growing shabbiness and inappropriate appearance. The uniform was his adumbration and represented his half-decent self, a faint image of Remembrance Sunday; it was the uniform Stella fell in love with in 1942, his flimsy protection to cover the horrible memory of Big John. He watched as cigar-smoking small-time gangsters assembled together to discuss their next heist in one room, while in the other, their women gathered in a dance led by Ginny. They danced until the early hours of the morning, listening to Stevie Wonder until the police were finally called by complaining neighbours and the drunk wedding guests disbursed.

London Docks

We sat in the front row stalls of the Electric Pavilion Cinema in Brixton to see the Beatles' first movie *Help!* That evening I was the gang mascot in a play of weight lifting, where each adolescent took it in turn to lift my small body horizontally overhead as we waited for the movie to start. The atmosphere choked on the golden smolder of marijuana being openly smoked by teenagers, including my brother's gang, who were ten years my senior. I thought the smell was truly repulsive and the numbness it installed in those around me painfully boring to watch. Another in the audience that night was Jimmy, my brother-in-law. He had just been released from prison the previous day and was making up for lost time by making a personal delivery of amphetamines, blues and speed fresh from King's College Hospital, to one of the faces in the crowd. The house lights dimmed and we took our seats in the packed Electric Pavilion, England's first purpose-built electric cinema, now England's biggest toke pipe of burning cannabis. The curtains parted and the movie rolled to the delight of the audience…

…An evil sect of brainwashed cult worshippers confronts Ringo in an Indian restaurant. Ringo learns that if he does not return the ring he wears to its rightful place he will become their next sacrifice. Ringo then discovers that the ring is stuck on his finger so they seek a jeweller to remove it, but the ring that holds a supernatural power breaks the tools the jeweller uses. In a desperate effort to remove the ring the band resorts to the clumsy efforts of a mad scientist, Foot, acted by Victor Spinetti, and his assistant, Algernon, played by Roy Kinnear. When his equipment has no effect on the ring Foot decides that he, too, must have it… and that's when it happened. During the song *You've Got To Hide Your Love Away,* the cinema became silent…

A silent giant moving image of John Lennon's lips fell across the screen. At first the audience thought it part of the movie as an eerie stillness filled the theatre. Some thought it a skillfully scripted piece of art, cleverly inserted into the storyline to give it more depth, greater meaning. After all, the Fab Four sported semaphore positions on the soundtrack album cover to the movie, positioning their bodies to spell out the word HELP. But then the house lights were switched on and the screen went dark. The manager came to the front of the auditorium flanked by two usherettes selling Player's Extra Strength cigarettes and melting vanilla ice cream.

"Ladies and gentlemen, boys and girls," he said, "I'm terribly sorry but we seem to have developed a mechanical problem. I can only assure you that we are doing our very best to resolve this as fast as possible so we can all continue to enjoy this evening's entertainment. I profusely apologise for this inconvenience." And with that he pushed the two usherettes toward the unhappy mob.

The appearance of the manager did little to sooth the anger of the mob and they started to throw rubbish at him. His conservative demeanour did little to win sympathy. A formal black DJ masked his stout figure, complete with a stiff-winged, starch coloured shirt and black bow tie. He looked like a snobby BBC radio presenter. Military style haircut flattened by hair oil and round turtle shell eyeglasses that gave him the appearance of being a snob and therefore legitimate game for the Brixton market workers in the audience to heckle him as was particular to that period. After five minutes people started walking out and demanded money back. Luckily, and despite their disappointment, the crowds were still in high spirits by England winning the FIFA World Cup the previous day, or else the cinema would have been trashed.

In due course the problem was identified. Unfortunately the projection booth also acted as the main ventilation flute and that evening the projectionist became intoxicated from the vast amounts of cannabis smoke being sucked his way. He was found stretched out on the floor in a catatonic state surrounded by a bundle of moving celluloid film unlacing itself from the second spool of *Help!* on the spinning projector.

After that I became the Beatles' biggest fan. My brother's group began to broaden their horizons using mind-expanding drugs to experience Brixton's psychedelic world so I avoided them as much as possible. Music was a huge part of my upbringing because song offered the promise of a better life, the escape of happiness. Vinyl was everywhere. The Beach Boys' *Good Vibrations* constantly played on Radio Luxembourg, transistor radios on every street corner – it was the feel good tune of summer. The sound of Paul McCartney's *Love Me Do* blasted through open windows echoing house to house, into school playgrounds and across Brixton Market, as distant but recognisable distortion. It was a sonic resonance that brought people together, in contrast to the 1960s brutal architectural vision of the future that isolated them.

Tower blocks and huge council estates were springing up everywhere to replace the Victorian slums destroyed by Germany's Luftwaffe V2 flying bombs that fell on South London from the skies only twenty years earlier. One day an estate appeared outside my primary school causing the intake of children to double in size. Suddenly strange kids that talked and acted differently surrounded me. Many were from the East End of London, others from Ireland, many from the West Indies. These children often came from troubled homes where families had been offered a fresh start in the new high-rise estates. The families had been relocated. The kids were tough and often beat frailer children, especially those inflicted by disfigurement. One such victim was Julian Smalley. Julian lived in a house directly next door to the school and his mother could look out from an upstairs window to see her child in the playground during break time. Julian's arched spine gave him a twisted appearance and his self-conscious walk made him a target. Children linked hands and ran in circles around him, like mini spectators in a diminutive freak show, until he would scream in fear. To compound his misery, Julian's parents thought it kind to purchase the house next door to the school, but this only made matters worse as his mother would watch from an upstairs window and weep to see her son treated in such a way. To this day I am still haunted by the child's piercing eyes that radiated a look that said *this world is not for me*. One lunchtime I tried to stop the bullies but I too became a target and was kicked to the ground. I simply accepted it, walked to the toilets and washed the blood from my nose in the washroom. I noticed Julian had locked himself in one of the toilet cubicles and was crying. The toilets were sanctuary for him. At that moment I knew school was not for me.

That afternoon I walked through the school gate to the Bricklayers Arms and sat on the step outside waiting for the afternoon stripper to finish her matinee. As the workmen finished their beer and started to leave I cupped my hands together and began collecting pennies from them like a beggar. I knew that these men were the fathers of the children who had just beaten me and I took a perverse delight in knowing they were paying for the sins of their children. I decided to leave before my mother came out and made my way to the corner shop to spend my bounty. Mr Fernhead was the shop owner. He took one look at my dishevelled appearance, grazed checks from the beating that I'd taken earlier, and asked where my parents were. I lied that both had died in a shipwreck of the Australian coast three weeks earlier leaving me to fend for myself. All I had in the world, I explained, were the few pennies in my hands.

"Poor little sod," said Mr. Fernhead. He then went about filling a huge brown paper bag with sweets until it was overflowing. I placed my pennies on his counter and he took them from me and replaced them with a pristine one pound note. My first experience at being deceitful had been a great success. Within the space of two hours I had accumulated massive sympathy, a small fortune and more importantly, learnt when to stop eating candy before being sick.

Despite my determination never to return to school, I was forced to later attend a comprehensive school, Kingsdale Comprehensive, where the same bullies joined me in the lower stream of non-academic aptitude and after four years all in that form failed the Certificate of Schools Education (CSE's). In one shocking incident I witnessed two of the more academic students from the upper stream being forced to perform fellatio in front of a gang of jeering thugs. I can still see the horrific look of humiliation and fear on their faces too. It shocked me then… it saddens me now. What are these bullies doing today? I wonder if they reflect back to that time and feel remorseful? Those boys, now men, were the offspring of the villains from Big John's fraternity of wickedness. Have they been tamed by comfortable middle class lifestyles, or are they still locked in a vicious cycle of devastation?

Tuesday afternoons were set aside for physical education and the most dreaded of days. Most students simply didn't bother turning up or failed to bring in their sports kit, choosing instead to be beaten by the teacher, otherwise known as "having the slipper." Yet again I was the focus of bullying and abuse, especially during showers or afterwards in the changing room. Sex, of course, was the reason. Many of the boys had already developed into their pubescent age, shaved their upper lips and had grown thick pubic hair with an adult voice to boot. My voice never dropped, ever.

For the more mature boys, one amusement to be had after showering was to openly masturbate in competition. This began by hanging wet towels over their erect penis, using it rather like a coat hook. The winner was judged to be the boy who could sustain the most towels for the longest period without their penis sagging. As time passed, the game developed a more extreme flavour with the boys showing little to no embarrassment. No one ever reported this homoerotic nonsense to either the teachers or housemasters through fear of peer retribution in the schoolyard or, even worse, after school hours when droves of adolescents moved en masse from school to bus stop, dredging for victims.

Although the school was multicultural, the West Indian children did not participate in this humiliating sideshow. Instead, they remained self-segregated and certainly knew never to shower or change their clothing in the presence of the white bullies. They displayed dignity that stretched beyond the boundary of the comprehensive and played cricket until the hooligans went home. How their experiences at Kingsdale, combined with the difficulties of being first generation immigrants, must have fuelled their hatred for authority. Kingsdale was a mixed comprehensive secondary school with an age range of 11-16 that opened in the 1952 and accepted close to 2000 pupils. During my attendance in the 1970s, it developed a reputation for poor performance and examination results until it was put under "special measures" in an attempt by Southwark Council to bring the school in line with the private school sector, such as Dulwich College, a fee-paying public school only a few hundred yards away. Be it the dreaming spires of a privileged education or the bicycle sheds of the comprehensive, life has taught me that respect is ultimately the abstergent force we all understand leading to success.

In November 1966 Victor took me to an East London gathering of merchant seamen on the Isle of Dogs. I remember it being November because it was Guy Fawkes Night, the 5th, and the sound of firecrackers exploding echoed across the damp night sky. It was a meeting of the Merchant Seamen's Union and the British Union of Fascists Shadwell and Rotherhithe Party held in the local community hall, normally used for Alcoholics Anonymous. The meeting gathered to listen to a speech being given by the conservative MP Enoch Powell. It was rehearsal to his now notorious, "Rivers of Blood" speech and the dangers of mass immigration, which he gave the following year in Birmingham. The high-voltage atmosphere was tense and my chest pounded with the sound of angry men shouting. The mix of men was noteworthy. Some wore white shirts, others looked like teachers, a few appeared as bearded beatniks in brown woollen turtleneck jumpers with elbow patches. One man in a black shirt wore an armband with a lightning flash design, the symbol of Oswald Mosley's diabolical group of fascists that had been disbanded after the "Battle of Cable Street." These were strongmen in their prime, trade union officials, dockers, merchant seamen and stokers from steam ships fresh with the smell of coal. Steam power was still alive with ample low-cost fossil fuel loaded into the boiler rooms of steamers by the ton. The docks faced mass unemployment and as the new container ships required the building of larger ports outside London, the cost of labour was forcing closure. Along the estuary toward the new modern dockyards of Tilbury and away from the East End, communities had formed generations of traditional industries, each depending on the docks for a living and immigration proved the scapegoat. Political idealists and Marxists spreading communist utilitarianism joined the meeting as my father heckled Enoch Powell with incoherent questions to the point where Powell asked his body guards to remove us.

"Give the coloured man a chance, all men deserve a chance!" he yelled.

Grabbing Victor by his lapel he was frogmarched to the door and pushed into the street.

"Get that leery poof out of here! Who the fuck does he think he is, dressed in that uniform? Go on, piss off home, you're not wanted here!"

I followed my father out into the soggy evening atmosphere. The smell of hemp sacks and coal from the ships clung to every surface and in that darkness my ears rang from the chants of politics and the swish of lapping water against the protruding jetty.

"You're a cunt," I said.

"What?' he said.

"I said you're a cunt."

I remembered the word being used by Big John the night he visited South Croxted. In my innocence, it seemed an appropriate word that summed up Victor. My father drew back his hand and knocked me to the ground. I got to my feet feeling numb, no pain, just a tingling sensation.

Victor turned and sat with his back to me on the wet sidewalk and buried his head in his hands. He looked up and said:

"Don't you ever call me that again or I'll kill you. As God is my witness, do you understand me? And never use that word in front of my mother."

I nodded and felt very confused.

Victor had a very odd relationship with his mother, Ethel. Somehow, mother and son were interwoven. When they kissed, it wasn't pleasant. It was more like they were lovers – not that anything like that happened, I'm sure, but it seemed they had an unhealthy relationship where everything else took second place. She doted on him and he on her every word and when she eventually died, he was absolutely beside himself. This, at least, was something Victor shared with Big John, for they both idealised their mothers. The eviction from the hall triggered his deep insecurity, and sadly, some hours later his frustration turned on me once again. By the time we returned home that evening, he had convinced himself I was turning into a girl. He stripped me naked and forced me to stand on a table at the centre of the kitchen under a light bulb and then began measuring me, starting with the length of my arms, the distance of my fingertips to the floor and leading to the length of my penis. My arms, he concluded, were far too long and my body was misshapen like a monkey's. The size of my penis was a matter of great concern to him, proving that I was, in fact, changing sex! I had become the embodiment of the word I had used on him, a cunt.

The next day, my mother promptly marched me off to the doctor's for an examination. The doctor concluded that I was a perfectly normal nine-year-old boy and my family had nothing to worry about. In fact, if anything, the doctor observed to my mother, I was a very strong boy.

"Martin's large kneecaps indicate he will grow to be a very tall chap indeed. There's absolutely nothing to worry about, Mrs Richardson, nothing at all, he's a perfectly normal child. Please don't concern yourself."

The doctor was right. At the age of sixteen I towered over Victor. His short stature prompted him to invest in a pair of handmade Chelsea boots with Cuban heels, the sort that have concealed insteps to provide an extra two inches of height. He wore these boots in public, especially when out with my mother. She was also taller than him so when standing next to each other they looked unevenly balanced, the odd couple. At parties when they danced to his favourite Perry Como recording of *It's Impossible,* he could finally look level into her eyes.

As I lay awake in bed at night listening to him I made plans for my revenge, knowing it was only a matter of time before his Cuban heels, and the haze of the 1960s, made way for my platform boots and the outrageous glam rock of the 1970s.

Lunar Footprints 1969

On 20 July 1969, Neil Armstrong took his giant step to make Apollo 11 history. I imagined myself an Apollo astronaut on a lunar mission... the eagle has landed.

We pose for my mother the photographer, who is about to take a photograph, our bodies fixed in an unnecessary act of freeze-frame, casting smiles that fell slowly as we held the pose for several seconds before she pushed the button. She was unsure what all the buttons on Cunningham's camera did so she carefully took her time. In the style of the period, I pose dressed in cream flannel trousers, a bright blue cotton bomber jacket with striped red and white elastic cuffs and a T-shirt with a CND peace logo. Uncle Lenny is also in the photograph together with his second wife, Margaret. We are sitting in the bright sunshine on a public bench by the seafront, eating ice cream in the coastal holiday resort of Rimini, Italy. Lenny had had the kind thought of taking us away from South Croxted after Big John's visit and the subsequent death of my grandmother, Henrietta, while Victor stayed at home. It was a perfect antidote.

It took three days for the Leyland Barnaby coach to travel from London to Rimini. The coach was winched onto the ferry at Dover. Then we sailed to Calais, where we walked down the gangplank to the awaiting Leyland, already winched off and ready to cross France. It was Calais to Rimini via Luxembourg and Switzerland, running up a total of 1,075 miles of scenic route. The open vista was beautifully picturesque, with mountain views that matched the wrapper of my Swiss chocolate bar. That coach was my rocket taking me away from Victor and the trepidation of the bullies at secondary school. We stopped at San Marino, the oldest recorded sovereign state and constitutional republic in the world. Now the centre of plastic religious tackiness, I loved its intensity. Eye-popping history was coming alive. I felt intoxicated by the sun and the vivacity of the Italian people took hold.

As we entered the old town of San Marino, the coach was lumbering up a steep gradient toward a holy monastery located at the mountain's peak when suddenly the engine came to a shuddering halt. A peasant farmer had delayed our advance by riding his donkey in the centre of the pass, refusing us passage despite our driver sounding the horn. The engine had overheated. After exchanging obscenities with the farmer, our burly driver jumped from the cab, grabbed the farmer by the neck, and attempted to strangle him. It was like an operatic scene from *Carmen*, that moment before the performance starts and one feels a poignant mix between reality and act. A violent fight for life ensued with the farmer striking back to give our driver a bloody nose, making our coach driver squeeze the farmer's neck even tighter, a true stranglehold, Big-John-style.

It was then that our guide, a charming English rose named Daphne, diplomatically parted them with a genial shrug, as if such fights were an everyday occurrence.

"Very passionate people, you know, very hot-blooded," she said. Displaying the perfect poise one might expect from a well-brought-up lady, with dignity and calmness she settled the scuffle by whispering into their ears that she would call in the *Carabinieri* unless they stopped immediately. The two men parted like abashed little boys. The farmer returned to his donkey that had watched the tangle from a hillside vantage point displaying a look of some amusement, and our driver returned to his packed coach of British ringside spectators, who offered Henry Cooper boxing tips.

Daphne's teeth were not her best feature. So large were they that when her lips parted, one noticed a red line running across them where her scarlet lipstick had smeared horizontally, leaving a bright pink landing strip that read like a dotted "cut here" instruction. After some minutes, passengers were requested to disembark and help push-start the coach. A middle-aged couple from Glasgow, dressed all in white, stood behind the exhaust just as the engine roared into action and a huge cloud of burnt diesel enveloped them, turning their immaculate white attire soot-black. British humour at its best, very *Carry On*. The couple had been together since childhood, so long in fact that one would start a sentence and the other would finish it. It had become an item of amusement within the coach group and the couple played to this, often adding a fake accent to their sentences that mimicked famous voices such as Sellers, Milligan and Bentine from *The Goon Show*. These sounds were comforting sounds, non-confrontational, in harmony. They each knew what the other was about to say before they said it, like predictive texting, but this was predictive thought, and all this made the slapstick violence of our driver and his ensuing humiliation somehow tolerable.

We eventually arrived at a family-run two-star hotel called "Ho el Italia." The letter "t" had fallen off "Hotel" so we called it "Hole Italia."

"Hole Italia" was a little piece of heaven and that afternoon I saw a movie being made in the lobby. Cameras followed a beautiful Italian blonde girl dressed in Paco Rabanne, a dress made entirely of gold chain, and below the links I could see her naked, tanned, body and blushed at the glimpse of her nipple. She was the most beautiful female I had ever seen, a goddess, my very own dream girl wearing nothing but a skimpy, provocative dress and white ivory bangles dangling from her wrists. The deep pink of her erect nipples kept me awake that night, and the exotic view of her fine pubic hair was breathtaking. That evening, I experienced the pang of my first orgasm and an erection that seemed to last for the rest of our holiday. I was twelve years old and she held everything life had to offer, everything except chocolate ice cream. I would never let Big John lay a finger on my dream girl. This was my lunar landing, my touchdown awaiting exploration in a sea of tranquillity, and I made a promise to myself that one day I would return to Italy and marry her.

The following morning, I went for an early morning walk and discovered a newspaper and cigarette kiosk selling my favourite ice cream, chocolate Galatia, and bought one. As I licked the melting brown goo in the morning heat, it dripped from my chin onto my clean top, causing a sodden mess. I looked up to see a young man walking toward me. His long wavy hair stood out. His eyes were strange, odd colours. He wore a T-shirt that carried the slogan: *I'm David Bowie, Aren't You?* It meant nothing to me, just another weirdo to be avoided. Later in life, as a fan, I discovered that he had in fact been in Italy during that time to promote *Ragazzo Solo, Ragazza Sola,* his Italian version of *Space Oddity.* This chance encounter with David Bowie was not to be my last. As a teenager, it was Bowie's music that set my mind free and turned South Croxted into a kaleidoscope of colour, a prophecy of what was to follow later in adult life.

"Hole Italia" employed a young male porter, Alberto, who took a shine to me. He was always smiling, extremely polite, and a brilliant draftsman. He pencilled from memory anything I asked him to draw and I sat for hours watching him and learning. It was like a magician's trick. I started spending my holiday allowance on art materials, paper and pencils, purchased from the corner kiosk, and would ask Alberto to draw my favourite cartoon characters and football heroes in their strip, which I would copy. At the end of our holiday, we rolled our drawings into a cardboard tube tied with a piece of string and he presented them to me as a farewell gift. These, I thought, were the best drawings in the world. I refused to have them packed with the rest of the luggage. Instead, I decided I would personally carry them back to London by hand for safekeeping. Our return journey was by train, and as we said our goodbyes I was tearful, for I knew what I was returning home to. At the station, we boarded our train to France.

The train compartment slept eight. The beds folded out into the centre of the carriage and towered vertically to a high ceiling. Three bunks high on either side, six per cabin. This mathematical certainty required sharing with two others, two strangers, a husband and wife who seemed over-attentive to each other's needs and took mysterious tablets and avoided conversation. *How could they sleep when there was so much to see and do?* I thought. I slid open the carriage window to inhale the rich smell of freshly ground coffee and take in the sights of the station as both diesel and steam locomotives entered and departed the giant glass structure.

As I watched all this, I accidentally dropped my treasured drawings from the high carriage window onto the station platform. I called for help, attracting the attention of a burly station cleaner, a large framed, unhappy-looking man with a cold stare. I was scared to leave the train in case it left without me, so I frenziedly pointed down toward the roll of Alberto masterpieces, begging the cleaner to pass them back up to me in my best sign language. Instead, he stared at them, stared back at me, raised his broom and swept them under the train onto the track below. They had gone forever. I have never trusted a station cleaner since and even today, I carry a strong mistrust for anyone holding a broom.

Len met Margaret while working for London Transport driving

buses. She took the fares as he drove and that was the way it was throughout their lives together – him driving as she held the purse strings. Their spell as £10 immigrants in Australia was short-lived; they moved back to Britain two years later due to acute homesickness. When they returned, Lenny trained to become a pub landlord and his new life started at The Prince Albert in Canning Town, a pub known to make or break a landlord.

It was here that he came into contact with many known criminals. Three years earlier, in 1966, Ronny Kray had walked into the saloon bar of the nearby Blind Beggar and shot George Cornell in the head, using a 9mm pistol. Some say that this happened because Cornell had called Ronnie a "big fat poof." Ron obviously took offence and sought revenge. However, according to reliable sources, it is more likely that the shooting occurred due to a business disagreement involving the Richardson Brothers, (that's another Richardson family – not mine!) This gave rise to a modern myth fuelled by the press that pubs in the East End were dangerous – and so they became dangerous.

One evening, however, Big John pulled a revolver out during a crowded drinking session and threatened to shoot him unless the barmaid stripped naked.

"You can't shoot me!" Lenny said. "I'm your Governor!"

That kind of front meant a lot in Canning Town and Big John found a respect for Len, so he put away his gun and left repentantly.

If you were working class in the sixties, it was virtually impossible not to come into the company of one sort of crook or another.

Above the brewery gates stood a giant sculpture of a golden rooster and the words, TAKE COURAGE, standing over a metre high. That's exactly what Stella did; she took courage with the 1960s London variants on the "'lonely men pay pretty girls for conversation" racket. Like Murray's Cabaret Pub where the Profumo Affair sex scandal girls, Christine Keeler and Mandy Rice Davies, worked as hostesses, The Bricklayer's Arms presented itself as cabaret, but the real draw was the more fatal combination of drink and femme hostesses.

The staff often circulated between places to meet gangster's trolls such as "Mad" Frankie Fraser, the Kray twins, the Richardsons and Big John. The pubs and clubs were aimed at the criminal fraternity, and were successful precisely because of the frisson created when high society and gayerati mixed with the "dangerous classes" of London's underworld. These risqué pubs' links to organized crime meant that girls who made their living this way didn't always have the most pleasant of working conditions. My mother worked hard as a barmaid without ever missing a shift and every afternoon she would sit in front of the mirror for hours, putting on her make-up, getting ready for the part. Curling her hair, painting on the foundation, then the eyes and finally her lips. Hair curlers, more foundation cream, eyeliner and lipstick until she looked like a Hollywood star. The mask was complete. At that moment, she was no longer my mum, or Stella, but a star. That's what Victor called her, "Star"…

She portrayed herself as a glamour model and photography provided that evidence. For a woman who found life tolerable only by staying on its surface, it was natural to be satisfied with offering the surface to others. Like all stars, she came out every night until daybreak, when her Cinderella painted mask was removed with morning cream and her face became the face of my mother again. Tender years languished as Victor remained in prison, thinking up alternative methods of wealth creation. Stella's bright hazelnut eyes, crimson lips and Kathy Kirby figure opened doors and turned heads, so when she was heavily pregnant with me, it must have been difficult for her. I was her third child, but not her third pregnancy. She sadly had several terminations in back street clinics before abortion became legal.

After the Big John incident, Lenny moved from The Prince Albert in Canning Town to the peaceful Cricketers in Mitcham, and finally to The Pilot on the windswept south coast of Romney Marsh, Dungeness. Its clientele were a very odd mixture of local crab fishermen, scientists from Sizewell "A" and "B", Britain's first nuclear power station, and a bunch of bohemian, gay, artist friends and lovers of the avant-garde filmmaker, Derek Jarman. Jarman owned an old fisherman's cottage nearby and was often found holding court in the saloon bar with my uncle in The Pilot. It seems they had found a kindred spirit in Dungeness, with its rugged beaches of stones and a scarcely populated sanctuary for all kinds of birds, a nature reserve and perfect isolation from the intensity of London, a last chance saloon. But it was the food that made it a popular stopping point for many. Margaret took to the kitchen and created one of the finest fish and chip restaurants on the South Coast, due much to the size of the locally caught fish. The jury is still out regarding why the fish are so large in that area. Some think it is due to low-level leakage of radiation from Sizewell. But a more likely explanation is the warm temperature of the surrounding seawater, for seawater is used to safely cool the nuclear fuel rods and is then sent back out to sea via an underground pumping system.

Now a widower, Lenny has retired from running The Pilot. He resides in his windswept bungalow on a shingle beach in an area known as The Marshes. It was here that Charles Dickens set the scene for Magwitch to escape the prison ship in *Great Expectations,* where Pip met his future fortune by feeding the escaped convict. Lenny's living room is a miniature version of a pub built from remnants of The Pilot after its current tenants refurbished it. Its bar is dotted with optics dispensing spirits, above which hangs a bell that once rang last orders. Circular beer mats neatly line the counter at regular intervals and long thin towels advertising lager protect its surface from imaginary customers. Beer bottles are stacked neatly on shelves, surrounded by distillery memorabilia, together with personalised framed embroidery celebrating his fifty years as a publican. Large patio glass doors look out to the Dungeness Lighthouse, the final stop of the famous Romney, Hythe & Dymchurch Light Railway, reopened after WWII in 1947 by Hollywood stars Stan Laurel and Oliver Hardy, and the lifeboat station where he was once an active volunteer. As he puffs away at another cigarette, he thinks of all this and longs for Margaret.

Leaving Croxted

A CHEQUERED JIGSAW OF POLYESTER ran the length of the hallway in Croxted Road. It was a rich embroidery made from carpet samples stolen from outside Carpets-R-Us on Streatham High Street. Hundreds of squares that together made a spectrum of floral motif, smooth interlay and flocked nylon relief neatly sewn together by Victor, with surgical skill. Every Saturday morning, he would vacuum it with such force that the aluminium nozzle became hot. Penetrative movements challenged nylon fibre; it was if he were trying to clean a bad memory, or even time itself. As Victor vacuumed, he swayed with the rhythm of a butcher chopping meat. Viewed from the back, this action, and his knock-knees, made him look like a gentle reprobate from *Toy Town*.

Beyond my bedroom window another world was waiting. I pulled the brown plastic grip from the mantel of the plywood wardrobe and slid my much-coveted Bowie album, *Ziggy Stardust,* flat in its base. I carefully folded my Levi 501s and neatly placed my white cap-sleeve T-shirt. I turned on my Sony Walkman to full-volume and listened to *Babylon's Burning* by The Ruts, took a deep breath, and started to walk the dreaded patchwork carpet along the hallway, passing Victor on my way through the tattoo door without so much as a word, to the bus stop where I boarded a number three. I sat on the upper deck of the old Routemaster bus and unwound one of the vented windows, outstretched my hand, and stuck two fingers in the air toward Victor. The Jamaican bus conductor said:

"Hey man, there's no need for that rudeness here, you know!"

An old lady joined in, "That's the problem with young people today, they've got no respect for elders!"

The bus drove me to an opening perspective, a vanishing point on the horizon of South London, directly into the heart of Brixton riot, toward a world in revolt. Stretched plumes of black smoke trailed the horizon, an acrid smoulder that could be seen by the Prime Minister, Margaret Thatcher from her parliamentary window in Whitehall. It was as if the whole world had become a revolting, violent overspill of South Croxted. I made my way to Electric Avenue, to the sounds of reggae music blasting from speakers the size of wardrobes outside the Cultureman Rastafarian Sound Shop. Amidst the anarchy, the only certain thing were the consumptive effects of cannabis grown in the backyard of a dealer's squat in Railton Road, locally known as "The Front Line," my new home.

The riot was triggered by the actions of two young PCs who

saw a man putting something in his socks and searched him on suspicion of carrying drugs. Although he protested that he merely kept his money in his socks for safety, they proceeded to search his car, and walked round it to check the tax disc and licence plates. To the small crowd that had gathered to harass the officers, this appeared as provocative authoritarianism. Violence broke out, eventually centring on Railton Road, where the police regained control only after many buildings and cars had been set alight and the fire brigade had been attacked. Many of the black youth were my friends from school – Clive Brown and his brother Errol, Raymond Frances and his cousins, kids I sat next to and knew, suddenly turned violent rioters. I, like so many of these young men fighting in the street, was disillusioned by school and maturing into a rebellious young man.

During the 1981 Brixton riot, 299 police were injured, and at least 65 civilians. 61 private vehicles and 56 police vehicles were damaged or destroyed. 28 premises were burned to the ground and another 117 damaged and looted. 82 arrests were made. Molotov cocktails were thrown for the first time on mainland Britain, and many of the adolescents I had been to school with engaged in the riot. There had been no such event in England in living memory.

Lord Scarman was appointed by the Home Secretary to hold a public inquiry. The report concentrated on the policing rather than the underlying causes of the riot, but made it clear that it was an outburst of violence against the police, and that local community leaders and police should share the blame for the breakdown in communications. It also stated that the police needed to be better organised for riot control, and made clear the extent to which increasing unemployment, coupled with discrimination against the black community in a variety of ways, were vital contributory factors.

★

In 1981 I took my first job with Lambeth Council as a gardener. Interviews took place at the gatekeeper's house of West Norwood Cemetery, with the option of choosing between grave-digging and gardening. I opted for "Council Path & Lawn Maintenance." The money was generous and I found a great congeniality between the men I worked with, especially a young man named Mark. Mark came from upright middle-class stock. He was born in the expensive part of Pimlico, sent to Eton as a boarder aged nine and expelled for smoking dope at fifteen. At sixteen, he ran away from his comfortable home to roam wildly in Brixton. At eighteen, he was working as a gardener. Despite his drug abuse, he was tall and athletic with long, dark, wavy hair and the brightest blue eyes that became searchlights when he smoked opium. He wore a red wife-beater vest, denim 501 Levi's and snow-white converse trainers. He refused to wear the standard issue gardening uniform like the rest of us, and was somehow allowed to get away with it.

Hygiene within the gang was not of primary concern. The obligatory Monday shave and clean workmen's overalls provided by the council degenerated long before Friday. The smell of body odour, freshly cut grass and tobacco mixed with the vapours of gasoline from the two-stoke lawnmower engines, creating a unique musk. During his inspection visits, the foreman could tell how hard the men had been working by the pungent nose of the odour. Members of the gang included a huge, strong, black Jamaican, Reggae Leroy, who never talked, slept when not moving and always, hot or cold, day or night, wore a heavy, black, oversized donkey jacket, the sort with leather shoulders and half-back rain protection.

During tea breaks and lunch hours, I started drawing my fellow workmates in their surroundings in the style of Van Gogh and Millet, artists who moved me. My heart melted when looking at their masterful charcoal drawings and paintings during my regular Saturday visits to the Tate Gallery in Pimlico. Paddy, an elderly Irish man, was constantly drunk and often immobile, making him a great figure for still life. His thin, wiry frame supported what can only be described as an outer shell, the inside of which had been dissolved by whisky long ago. There was Bald Head Pete, the half-wit, a delightful man who had the mind of a child and was always the figure of fun for Ginger Paul, the gap-year sociology student writing up his PhD thesis on The Group Dynamic – perfect subject matter. Finally, there was Tiny Tim. He dealt drugs and it was through Tim that I found my temporary home in Railton Road.

Anyone who has ever lived in a squat will understand what I mean when I use the term "living in uncertainty." Life becomes temporary. One fends for oneself because the law is not there for you. I was totally at the mercy of others' benevolence, people who demanded respect with no juncture for friendship. Truth was currency. Food was something of a luxury and that year my bodyweight reduced by three stone. I only ate oats and raisins as sold by the emerging health food shops, then called Community Shops, who offered a free cup of herbal tea with every purchase. I saw the other side of respectable society emerging under the cover of darkness, the middle-class sons and daughters of bank managers, solicitors even the clergy, who visited our squat to buy illicit drugs. This started with a coded knock at the toughened door, whereby reinforcements were loosened to an opening of only a few inches. Six-inch screws had been driven into the floorboards to stop any door opening further, thus eliminating the threat of forced entrance by the police, who would be restricted by cumbersome body armour, shields and helmets. Druggies, however, could squeeze through the narrow gap easily, to shuffle along the darkened passage piled high with litter, into the front room that seemed an oasis by comparison. Its clean, minimalist décor of wooden floorboards and boarded windows made the house a medieval keep.

Each night, I sat beggar-like in the corner of the room, studying the punters. One by one, they arrived to collect and pay. Young, middle-class, respectable-looking folk, mainly female, arrived every thirty minutes to buy hash, speed or coke. Tim's twin brother, Axel, had set up shop a few doors down and only sold smack. Tim operated scientific scales, an indication that he was honest and you would never be sold short. He measured out quantities exactly to order and made it a rule never to give credit over £100. There was a penalty for people who paid late, Axel would see to that. He had been ripped off far too many times to be lenient. The twins' deceased mother was a crackhead and the twins knew no different. They had been born into this lifestyle, they knew nothing better in life and, for all these misgivings, they were sharp businessmen. Tim could be a high roller in the city today for all I know, determining others' fates just as he did then, with a razor-sharp judgment. There was a racial element to this drug-dealing system, for the suppliers were protected by organized crime, who cosseted the squat. The left side of the street – even numbers – was predominantly confined to whites. The right side of the street – odd numbers – was predominantly black and protected by the Jamaican bad men, the Yardies. My enemy's enemy is my friend, a collective abhorrence for law and order.

One night, Donovan visited us from Sheffield. He was one of the older squatters, in his early thirties. He had just been to see Axel, no doubt for a gram or two of heroin. He was a user, the type who always dressed in faded denim loons and denim cowboy shirt. He had long grey shoulder-length hair tied in a ponytail, like Francis Rossi of Status Quo. Donovan had systematically worked his way through the various types of drugs, treating these classifications as an academic pursuit. He had been educated, but dropped out of UCL while studying chemistry as an undergraduate student. On this particular night, he joined us and sat in a dark corner as the main group sat in a large circle listening to Pink Floyd's *Atom Heart Mother*. Time passed and people started to leave, all except Donovan, who appeared to be sleeping.

Tim went over to him and gently shook his arm in order to wake him. "Come on, mate, time to go out," but Donovan slumped face first onto the heap of roaches assembled in the ashtray.

"Fuck me, he's dead!" said Tim. "The cunt's gone and snuffed it in my pad. What am I supposed to do now?"

"Take him down the pub," said Frances, who was about as high as possible without passing the limit of consciousness.

"Good idea," said Tim and, pulling the corpse to its feet, Donovan was dragged out of the house. Moments later, they entered the public bar of the Atlantic pub just in time for last orders. In one careful movement, Tim sat the body onto the wooden bench next to the gents. It was like a scene from Saint-Saëns' *Dance Macabre*. Meanwhile, Frances returned from the bar, placed three pints of Special Brew before them and started a fictitious conversation with the corpse.

"Sorry you're not feeling too well, mate, but it serves you fucking right for being such a greedy bastard. What's that? You want to have a piss? Well, you'll just have to wait a few more minutes until we've finished our beers."

The beers were lined up in front of the corpse and Tim and Frances drank quickly. The corpse did not. After a few moments, they slowly made their exit, leaving the corpse with his pint. The manager of the Atlantic was in for a shock and as the old seafaring bell rang to sound last orders, the pint still stood untouched.

"Time gentlemen, please!" yelled the manager.

On realising things were not kosher, the staff apparently dragged Donovan's body outside into the street and sat it against a lamp post for police to discover. After all, the dead were bad for business. We thought that was the last of Donovan, but later sightings suggested that he had returned to Sheffield the following morning, none the worse.

It was during this time that my cousin, Robert, was killed in a motorbike accident at the tender age of sixteen. His body was taken to a firm of undertakers whose establishment was adjacent to the gatekeeper's house in West Norwood Cemetery, so during my lunch break I took the opportunity of visiting Robert before he was buried. His body was already bloating from the intense summer heat that speeded the enzyme reaction of decomposition. Gas had built up within his putrefying body and he appeared a greenish hue.

Mark was most insistent that he came along, saying how badly he had always wanted to see a dead body but had never had a chance. So it was from macabre curiosity that we entered the cold, darkened Chapel of Rest. His bloated corpse was unrecognisable. I don't think one ever gets over the shock of seeing a dead body. Mark and I stood transfixed, staring at Robert for what seemed like hours. Then suddenly Mark started to make odd wailing noises in sheer terror. He was having a trip, a flashback from acid he'd taken several nights earlier. In his mind's eye, Mark could see the corpse's head slowly turning, opening its eyes and looking directly towards him. Mark ran from the Chapel of Rest screaming in terror, convinced my zombie cousin was about to follow him.

During one of his rare lucid moments, Mark said, "Once you have broken free of the bullshit rules made up by an uptight society in a fucked-up world, the police become the focus of your hatred. They represent power and repression. In a squat, nothing except the present matters, not even death, because you have a freedom very few can imagine."

THE IRA'S BLOODY REVENGE

Lieutenant-General
Sir Steuart Pringle

Brave Marines chief is hit by bomb

Blitzed . . . the wreckage of the general's car after it was blown against a parked Rover by the bomb

THE BLAST that maimed one of Britain's top soldiers yesterday was a brutal act of IRA revenge.

By Sunday People Reporters

is chief of the Royal Marine Commando Forces.

The Commandos played a key role in arresting IRA

IRA hard-liners have sworn they would get their own back.

And yesterday they did.

Eye-witnesses praised the general's courage after the bombing.

One said: "He was brave, very brave."

Last night the general, a Roman Catholic and

£10,000 BINGO

Shapes on Late Night Television 1981

$1$7ᵀᴴ OCTOBER 1981, MY BIRTHDAY. A cold north-westerly air stream sweeps across London from Siberia. In South Croxted my parents' neighbour, Lt General Steuart Robert Pringle, leaves home for his usual drive to work in his Rover 500 army executive limo. He is about to become the victim of a booby-trap explosion caused by the tilting of a mercury trigger connected to Semtex under his car. As a result, he will be seriously injured with the loss of a leg. Miraculously his Labrador, "Bella" who travels with him, survives without a scratch.

Victor attempts to thumb a lift from his neighbour to escape from the biting wind. At that very moment, the explosion lifts the car from the ground and blows Victor into the air, propelling him across the street and into the front garden of number 89. After a few seconds, he stands up. He is suffering from shock and returns to the General's car to find the General screaming in silence. Victor has been made temporarily deaf from the shockwave of the combustion and suffers the embarrassment of having had both his trousers and his underpants torn from his legs. He stands, penis exposed, naked to the world and dripping blood, then passes out. The General is not screaming in pain but warning others not to approach the vehicle, for it was common IRA practice for two bombs to detonate, one a few minutes after the other for maximum destruction.

The emergency services attend. Victor regains consciousness on a trolley parked in a corridor inside the casualty ward of King's College Hospital. Falling in and out of consciousness, he dreams a sedated dream of the perfect crime.

On the other side of London, I'm celebrating my birthday. I show Mark the drawings that I made the day before in a life class for which I had enrolled at Camberwell School of Art. We sit on his bulky sofa salvaged from the yuppie skip and smoke copious amounts of cannabis, giggling, munching on peanut butter sandwiches washed down by ice-cold lager and cocaine chasers to celebrate my 21st birthday. Mark reaches for the TV remote as a news flash flickers horizontally, a zigzag of confusion from the screen and that's when I see it: South Croxted has been destroyed.

It's dawn. Although my head's still buzzing from the effects of narcotics and alcohol taken hours earlier, I know I need to reach the emergency blue and white stripy plastic ribbon that cordons South Croxted, with a sign on it saying: *POLICE – NO ENTRY*, a Mobius strip, one side life, the other death. Bored uniforms dot the wide street, each wanting to go home to a warm bed. They wish they were anywhere but at the scene of this crime and who could blame them? Shortly after I arrived, the tallyman drove to the cordoned-off road in his sky-blue three-wheeled Reliant Robin Deluxe and, on seeing the devastation, made a U-turn without slowing down, almost causing an accident as his tri-car nearly overturned.

"What a fucking way to make a living!" he murmured under his breath.

He was one of life's unfortunate people who consistently turn up at the wrong place at the wrong time at exactly the point when they are unwanted. *I've had enough of this shit,* he thinks to himself and points his small car north.

Meanwhile, avoiding the police standing guard, I had managed to find a way into our house. A Siberian breeze soughs through the nylon curtains, through my stoned haze, sobering my thoughts, and I see the results of the car bomb. Jimmy's rented canary yellow Ford Cortina Estate lay crumpled like a crushed wrapper, thrown against the bus stop... the tarmac of South Croxted blackened and dented by the force of the blast. A forensic marquee has been erected, glowing with light from within like an extraterrestrial craft, making clear its intentions for the warring worlds, illuminating the blood splatters on the pavement and York stone kerbs. General Pringle's car has become a convertible, its roof blown from its chassis, pimped by the IRA bomb.

The stench of Semtex still lingers in the chilled evening air, a strange smell of almond marzipan and methane. I hear human noises coming through the thin plasterboard wall, repetitive muffled beating sounds. In the mirror, I see a reflection of a man jerking off in my mother's bedroom. It's Casey, repulsive, farting and coughing simultaneously as he reaches orgasm, as if in some vile, illegal vaudeville performance. Once he's finished jerking, he wipes his hands on the bedclothes and then folds them to hide the wet sperm. Zipping his fly, he stands and smiles, then places his hands behind his back, a gesture of self-importance. He appears pleased with himself as he moves from room to room, pulling small, embedded pieces of shrapnel from the wooden slatted ceiling and plasterboard walls like a monkey picking fleas. I keep reminding myself that I must not be found, just as I did as a child when I hid from my parents and brother and sister. "Noble restraint, noble restraint," I repeat over and over again as I fight the urge to punish him for his disgusting disrespect. His inane smirk makes me feel uneasy and if I were not curious to see what happened next, I would take great pleasure in hitting him. A forensic Sherlock Holmes, one eye on the evidence, the other on his notebook, his scarred, ravaged, pocked cheekbones balance the biological causality of cruel testosterone. His body smells of the unloved, unwashed. His alien eye sees his way downstairs to Victor's room and I follow, to find him rifling through typed documents and carbon copies until he finds the gun. The same gun that I played with as a child, the gun Victor took to kill Big John, the gun Victor was given as a sample from the shipment destined for Samuel in Africa. Uniformed policemen enter the room, a double act, passing the gun to each other like a hot potato, to and fro, to and fro.

Now it makes sense. The Congo affair, the authorities diverting the arms shipment, including Semtex, to Libya, who in turn trained The Irish Republican Army in the gentle art of bomb-making and small arms fire. All this took place under the guise of the Met Police Training Diplomatic Department. It was the British authorities that offered services to Libya, to train the diplomats that ultimately killed PC Fletcher, shot dead outside the Libyan embassy in London after agreeing that any Libyan diplomat involved in violence would be judged in Libya, not in the UK. Without Libya, the IRA would have been unable to plant the bomb that rocked South Croxted in an attempt to assassinate Lt General Steuart Robert Pringle.

By a twist of fate, or karma, Victor was intrinsically linked with the events that led to the explosion – an event that ironically levitated him to the front pages of the world's press, where the measure of cities, like the measure of friendship, cannot be encompassed by events unless that event is beyond belief. The British *Daily Mirror* headline called Victor a "Real Local Hero," as he was prime witness to the bloody affair. How strange life can be and how incredible. And to extend this incredulous story even further, we need to consider DC Casey, the sleeping IRA extremist, the only person that could have possibly masterminded such an elaborate chain of events and walked away squeaky clean and intact. Could this bizarre scenario be true?

On 12 March 1994, some thirteen years after the bomb, Victor died in his sleep from a heart attack, aged 72. It was only in later life that he underwent several major operations for stomach hernias, which no doubt owed much to my brother's trusty blows from years earlier, and several heart bypasses later, he was dead. It was after his first heart bypass operation that one could hear his chest tick like a clock, as titanium valves opened and closed with the pumping of blood, like the salutary clock ticking inside J M Barrie's crocodile.

When my mother discovered his body, she also found hundreds of photographs surrounding his deathbed, carefully assembled to make a photographic timeline. This final act was overlooked by all but me, for the shock of his death concealed any meaning this arrangement may have had. I gathered the photographs away from his corpse and placed them into plastic carrier bags. They are my prompt for this book. By weaving together truth and deception in life, he remained deluded unto death, the final truth. A metaphysical Mr Wonderful documented through photography, mementos of a life that forged another truth. In death, he was cremated in his uniform, like a Viking passage to his other world. My brother Raymond and his wife Lesley took it upon themselves to edit Croxted Road's history by destroying many of the counterfeit papers and documents found in Victor's study, sadly without consultation. As playwright Alan Bennett once said, "It's an odd family that censors its own history, and it's that which makes it interesting."

Victor's was a hearty feast, and from that hearty feast only crumbs remain.

FRANK*land* 2012

How deep do I go to lose you,
how high do I climb before you fall?

Hmp Frankland is an impressive building standing thirty metres high by five hundred long. Its minimalist façade contrasts
with the delicate landscape between Newcastle and Durham,
land purchased by Edward Heath's government in the early 1970s
ceasing any suburban new-town expansion to instead construct
Europe's largest top-security "A" class prison. It contains men
such as Big John, still a detainee after all these years and now
close to death. The only clue to this once having been new-town-
land is a solitary house, a former "show home," now decompos-
ing opposite the main prison entrance. It reminds me of a town
constructed by American army engineers, never to be occupied
by real people, in the deserts of Nevada just outside Las Vegas,
home to the Atomic Testing Commission in the late 1950s, early
'60s. I feel like one of the test mannequins about to experience

the effects of the blast to come. The entire landscape evokes an eerie feeling that something is about to happen.

During the last decade, the prison population statistics for lifers, convicts incarcerated for murder in the United Kingdom, has risen from 4,000 to 14,000, a figure higher than all the other European countries combined. Frankland offers shelter to the most dangerous. Originally opened in 1980 with four wings, each holding 108 in single cells, a further two wings opened in 1998. These are in an open gallery design, to hold an additional 206 and a specialist Dangerous and Severe Personality Disorder (DSPD) unit. Here, the DSPD lost souls reside; the final rung of the ladder that ends in psychiatric isolation, where only medically-induced zombies remain of once high profile murderers, terrorists and child killers, the dammed "A" list. Mandatory life sentence was introduced for all murder convictions when the death penalty was abolished in England, Wales and Scotland in 1965. Since then, former inmates at HMP Frankland have included the longest serving prisoner in British legal history, serial killer John Straffen; Scottish Glasgow-born gangster and murderer, Paul John Ferris; London-born gangster and kidnapper, John Frances Fowler; that infamous serial killer of the elderly, Dr Harold Shipman; and Charles Bronson, the Welsh criminal often referred to in the British Press as "the most violent prisoner in Britain." Current inmates include child killer Ian Huntley, who killed ten-year-old schoolgirls Holly Wells and Jessica Chapman, along with Dhiren Barot and Hussein Osman, both of whom are of the al-Qaeda persuasion.

Truth to tell, I am neither trained nor mentally capable of

understanding these minds, apart from engaging at a social level more than any other man. However, I can pass judgement on their academic submissions and that is the reason I am here. My arrival gathers an earthly pace as I begin reading prison service magazine, "The Walden," a human side of the service.

I have a somewhat macabre interest in meeting a man who has taken the life of another, the thing most precious to all. This is a reflection of my formative years, when so many of the figures I encountered during my childhood revelled in the potential of violence. Violent times. During today's visit to Frankland, I must execute my role as a University External Examiner, to decide if the two prisoners who have opted to take classes have reached a level deemed academically suitable for degree status. I am reminded of the old dictum, "The pursuit of knowledge leads to money, the pursuit of money leads nowhere." I do not fear the prospect of entering the prison. I have the perspective of a prisoner's family, for I am, after all, the son of a convicted criminal, seed of an unlawful father.

The guard takes my fingerprints. My eyes are scanned for biometric identification and then my portrait photograph is taken. Personal details are checked, address, age, nationality etc., to be stored digitally on the Central Police Database register. My particulars are printed onto a lurid plastic card and embossed with a number and the word VISITOR, courtesy of the UK taxpayers. At Central Clearing I empty my pockets of personal belongings, mobile phone, watch, and wedding ring and am strip-searched.

A Geordie character sings, *Fly Me To The Fucking Moon*, a variation on the Tony Bennett standard, and jokes with the staff as heavy metal doors slam and echo along the cold concrete corridor, where a turning key tells its tale. I enter a revolving door into Holding Area No. 3, and then pass through a whole body scanner, after which I am frisked, spread-eagled. I'm questioned: "Where are you from? Why are you here? Who are you goin' to see?"

Eventually, I am processed to Level No. 4 clearance, where guards seem good-humoured despite news of the so-called "Facebook Killer'" Peter Chapman, having had his face mutilated and slashed by a fellow inmate the previous night, and the threat of a pending riot caused by an attack on inmate Malcolm Cruddas, who suffered horrifying injuries when terrorist Omar Khyam poured a pan of boiling chip fat over his head. It left Cruddas's face bubbling and swelling like a balloon and came after al-Qaeda dirty bomber Dhiren Barot was targeted in the same way.

Enclosures within enclosures, lock after lock, the security tightens as fences change from razor wire to electric wire, powered by a buzzing overhead current. Another fish net made from titanium strands stretches across the courtyard sky to foil aerial escape. Gates with inch-thick iron bars made from World War II army surplus make the high walls of D-Wing impenetrable.

"We stop when they move, we move when they stop," said Derek, my guard.

"Get it? That way, the cameras know who's where and why, get it?"

"Got it," I say.

Overhead cameras follow our progress, spaced out every few metres, performing a weird mechanical dance between the gates.

They turn horizontally, vertically, up and down in a true waltz of madness.

"Here's the workshop, a nifty short-cut... but not to worry," said Derek. "Staff take this short-cut all the time and have never had a problem."

"I guess that's alright then," I murmur.

As I follow Derek through the workshop, I can see inmates toiling over small benches, creating kitsch *objects d'art* – crudely painted depictions from *Looney Tunes* cartoons; gifts for children made by violent prisoners. Next, we come to a classroom where broken consoles and monitors pile ceiling-high, looking as if they could be an entry for the Tate Turner Prize, though they are, in fact, evidence of yesterday's tumult and frustration taken out on the nerds. No Internet here. No CD/DVD recording and copying or USBs used to dispatch or receive information to or from the outside. The appearance of information technology without information; an assemblance without function, making it an illusion.

Soulful Isaac Hayes look-alikes, sporting polished scalps with ludicrously large dark sunglasses, lurch theatrically across the blue office furniture at the far end of the room. They watch me as one might watch a menacing intruder and I feel intimidated. These black brothers surround an elderly white man. His face appears to be a well-preserved specimen from the 1960s, white roots showing from under a thatch of jet-black dyed hair. His face is very familiar to me, but for now, I can't place it...

My guard takes me to the classroom where staff are expecting me. I'm introduced to two mature female tutors, both the better side of fifty, and then to the Frankland inmates, Brian and Tim. Both have blue eyes of steel, as if a blinding light had long ago bleached away any trace of the colour surrounding the windows to their souls.

"Right, who's first?" I say, and I wave my arm only to realise that, in my absent-mindedness, I'm still wearing my expensive Seamaster Omega wristwatch, the timepiece I didn't wear for six months after purchasing it through fear of mugging, the watch I had saved up for to pamper my James Bond pretensions, justifying it through working hard and late nights in my office. The watch I forgot not to wear into prison...

"Brian first," says the warden.

Brian has gathered his paintings together for me to view. These are organised into a small exhibition that occupies one corner of the room. Brian's large face cradles the glint of a distant smile. He offers a jolly take on the proceedings and shakes my hand as if greeting an old friend, in a grip that is firm and sincere.

"Nice watch you're wearing," he says, with a smile.

"Thanks," I say.

His tombstone teeth have stature, not unlike the teeth of my friendly milkman embarrassed to ask for payment of his bill. Better start concentrating on the work, I think. It is a collection of cardboard cut-outs, small models of his prison cell. In it rest a pack of tiny playing cards. Some appear spinning through the door, others are flying over the prison landing balcony and into a large hole in the floor. One side of the playing card has been mirrored with silver foil, to reflect hidden messages scrawled on the walls of this tiny model room. One can read his date of birth, the name of his first school, a description of his first job, the army, etc., leading to his incarceration at Frankland together with his seventy-year-old father, Bernard.

He says that the "important thing" is that his art has helped him make sense of the past. He tells me about the sculpture:

"It's called *The More You Take, The More You Leave Behind,* just like footsteps, really. Thirty-two cards, thirty-two years old, that's me."

I search for the logic. Brian has been sentenced to life imprisonment for the cold and merciless killing of a teenaged boy who had witnessed Brian and his father holding up the local post office at gunpoint. The kid had decided to call the police from his mobile telephone and, during their getaway, Bernard ordered Brian to stop and deal with the boy. Brian did as his father had ordered and shot the scared teenager point blank in his face, blowing out his brains with a .22 handgun.

Other artworks by Brian include a series of paintings of lesbian sex scenes, all of which are apparently very popular with the other prisoners. For me, however, his most disturbing image is a painting of interference on the surface of water. Liquid by shape and form, but with no manifestation of light, no shining surface, just a dull, matte shape. A dull, rolling hillside rather than ripples on water. No sparkle or glint, no shine, no expression. The image seems to absorb light, like the mirror in Bram Stoker's novel, *Dracula*; no reflection. I can see Brian looking over my shoulder. I feel chilled by his art. Time to move on to the next inmate…

At first glance, one could easily mistake my second candidate, Tim, as a fellow academic, even a doctor, for he has the look of a surgeon about him. Tim looks very studious sitting at a draftsman's desk, using a fine brush to finish a detailed study of a still life, until he stands to greet me, and I now see he has the well-defined shape of a bodybuilder from working out every day lifting weights. Camp-looking young men hover near him and I can't help but wonder if they are they his lovers?

Tim takes off his round, wire-framed spectacles and walks slowly toward me. Like Brian, Tim's eyes have no pupils, only a distant cobalt shine. He talks quietly, in detail, about his 23 hours a day, seven days a week lock-in, about his last seven years in non-contact segregation unit as he posed an exceptional risk, and how art saved his life... possibly the lives of others, too.

"You're looking tired," Tim says. "Have a late night?"

I explain the disruption I was forced to suffer the previous night in my hotel, with doors slamming non-stop from a boozed-up wedding reception occupying the rooms on either side.

"Where's that then?" he asks.

"The Thistle," I reply.

His muscular shape slowly turns to face me and he says, "I know The Thistle, and I know exactly where you're staying..."

He says this not in threat, but as if a light is illuminating a dark place in his mind-map that he hasn't walked for ages. He leads me from one abstract painting to another, each one a black and white composition becoming increasingly asymmetrical and bizarre, like badly drawn fractals or incorrect mathematical equations.

"Do you have titles for them?" I ask.

"They're all called *Torment.*" He looks at me with an annoyed expression, as if he can't understand why I couldn't guess.

"How do you get your work seen as an artist?" he asks.

"Well, that depends," I say. "Today, a lot of artists have websites and show their work on the Internet."

"The Internet? What's that?"

"Well, the Internet was invented by Tim Berners-Lee. It allows your computer to communicate with other computers around the world in a network," I explain.

"A network? Just like television? A-fucking-mazing! Computers networking."

One of the young men shouts to Tim from across the room. "Oh, Tim! Terry's got another joke about Big John. How do you make an old puff pastry? Answer: with seven black heavies carrying rolling pins!"

The room combusts with spontaneous laughter and even the guard can't resist a smile. I'm not sure how I should react, as I remind myself that Tim had an extreme reaction to the death of his homosexual father Eric, aged 81, on Christmas Day 1990, before killing his mother. During the funeral, Tim was overtaken by an overwhelming desire to enter the grave during Eric's burial, wishing for them to be buried together.

A speaker hanging over the door starts to pulsate with a loud buzzing sound and a guard cries out, "One o'clock, back to your cells." With that, Tim leaves me as if he had been switched off. No goodbyes, he simply walks away, trailed by three effeminate young men.

Over tea, I ask the staff about Tim...

"Well, how can I put it?" says the senior psychiatrist, adding another spoonful of sugar to his already over-sugared tea. "Tim had lived an apparently normal life, existing alone with his mother, until one evening he decapitated her with a pair of small nail scissors. Nobody knows why he did it, although I think you were told about the trauma caused by the accidental death of his father. He's never shown any remorse and is clearly a lucid fellow, so they sent him to Frankland."

"That's horrendous!" I say, dipping another milk chocolate digestive into my already sweet tea.

"Yes it is. But the important thing is, after today, when you return home, home to enjoy your freedom, your family, your sanity... that you think yourself lucky."

The psychiatrist was, of course, correct and indeed I now have a better understanding of the Stockholm syndrome – that cognitive transactional trust which develops through the duration of the prisoner relationship, a procedure formed not with fear, but with friendship. When the prisoners challenge authority, the wardens engulf it, they enjoy it. It's a relationship that deals with very basic human compulsion for violence, acknowledging the fact that violence is often caused by those born of violence. The bullied become the bullies, and this, in a principled context, offers insight as to the nature of the beast. I also have a better understanding of the constraint of prison, but not what makes someone want to become a prison officer, or for that matter, what drives someone to be a criminal. A penchant for control, maybe? A pertinacious craving from the deepest recesses of the psyche? What makes one man good and the other man bad? Do we have choice? The law, together with religion, would argue that we do. Science and genetics would argue we do not.

On the train back to London, I reflected on the day… on the significance of penal servitude and its long-term effects on society, especially on its children. One face kept returning to my mind, the face of the old man in the IT lab, the face of my past, John Frances Fowler—Big John, the face that will haunt me forever. Now in his eighties, he was imprisoned until death's release in a place where time had stopped, and my luxurious Omega Seamaster timepiece held no value.

Both guards' and prisoners' names have been changed.

★ ★ ★

Starting

In 1990 I made a hologram of Lord Longford. We met at his Chelsea flat before driving to my studio in West London where the hologram was to be recorded and I was delighted to find his wife, Elizabeth Lady Longford CBE, had decided to join us as she was recognised as one of the finest biographers of her age. During conversation they enquired about my family, my past and my thoughts about prison reform without them knowing anything about my personal history; it was as if they had somehow sensed my background. At that time public opinion was against Longford's views with newspaper headlines galvanising his plea for a more humane rethink on prison sentences. He was demonised in the press for championing the early release of the Moors Murderer, Myra Hindley.

I told them I thought that prison for less serious crimes often harmed the families of the guilty as much as it punished those who committed the crime, and went on to tell them something of my own experience. They liked that. They also liked the idea of seeing a holographic duplicate, but struggled with the vanity to which portraits are often associated.

"You should write a memoir," he said.

"Find the truth," Lady Longford commented.

I remember my eyes drifting from his face to hers as the thought of it filled me with terror. I couldn't think of anything more ominous than to tell the world about my past, fearing it would cause further unhappiness and humiliation, even my professional doom. It did however leave an impression, and in the silence of the moment it came to no conclusion until now.

Victor's Study

Victor's study had a huge, round, Victorian oak dining table with carved lions' legs with huge, protruding, outstretched claws that drew together to project up to a central column. A weighty black die-cast Remington typewriter rested on top, heavy enough to make the table sway when being pounded by Victor's strong fingers. The Remington rested on a horsehair mat to protect the table's French polished surface, but which assisted its slide from one side of the table to the other. It was a visual joke from a silent movie, but then the house was a set for a trite comedy. At night, I would sneak into the room to hide beneath the table's mighty mantle as Victor occupied his distant world. I hid against its giant stalk, listening to his typing and the record which played John Barry's musical masterpiece, *From Russia With Love*.

The film, *From Russia With Love,* is filled with a heavy dose of non-stop action and adventure, and has an intelligent plot that comments heavily on the state of world affairs in 1963. Capitalists and communists are set to work against each other by SPECTRE, an organization which does not give any special considerations to economic systems, but wishes to weaken the balance of world power and take control itself. There are great acting performances from Sean Connery, Robert Shaw, Pedro Armendariz, and Lotte Lenya (the wife of Kurt Weill). I knew that one day I would visit Russia, as he never could.

Sam's Junk Shop
Sam's Junk Shop was located in one of Lambeth's worst slum areas. It was demolished in the 1980s, together with its surrounding streets, to make way for one of Europe's largest housing estates, Summerleyton. The building presents a long, impenetrable wall to the outside world and remarkably, it is today labelled London's most dangerous ghetto for knife crime. The dark force is still at work.

Dreams
As a child, I often dreamt I was running in slow motion. Taking giant leaps, which covered meters rather than feet, as if walking on the moon's surface. In the dreams I felt as if I were moving through sticky treacle and yet I was still able to run further and faster than others. To dream you are moving in slow motion

symbolises powerlessness, an immobilising stress and a need to flee. Dreams do not occur by chance; every thought is motivated by our unconscious at some level. Sigmund Freud believed that in order to live in a civilised society, we needed to hold back our urges and repress our impulses. In most cases they have a way of coming to the surface in disguised forms and one way these urges and impulses are released is through our dreams.

In Big John's case, however, the content of his unconscious was extremely disturbing and totally unsuppressed. In Victor's, his sanity was traceless. His dreams leaked into his consciousness, where the impulses and desires were no longer suppressed. Through his actions, we are able to get a glimpse into his hidden desires, which were so disturbing and psychologically harmful that every aspect of his fantasy encroached on my predicament. My father took a delight, as is common with most criminals, in destroying the dreams of others.

Crystal Palace

The BBC Television transmitting mast at Crystal Palace imposes a colossal 640 feet over this part of South London. In the early sixties, its grounds played host to a world famous road racing circuit. I can remember going to see motorcar racing with my brother one summer and feeling sick from the deafening roar of the engines. Later, it became a meeting point for teenagers who gathered under the mast's heavy, Eiffel Tower-like base to drink pale ale and smoke pot. In 1969, it became the location used in the movie *The Italian Job*, starring Michael Caine. It was here that criminal mastermind Caine introduced his henchmen to the new Mini Coopers for a training session before the stunts in Rome. The scene was filmed just under its spectre of a mast and six years later, when I was old enough to drive, I learnt on that very same piece of tarmac, leased by a canny businessman who spotted a marketing angle for the motor trade of would-be Michael Caines.

Victor's Childhood

My father's real name was Victor Walter Charles Biddlecomb. Later, after my birth, it changed again, from Richardson to Lion-heart-Riechardson, giving it a noble Germanic ring that served him well when working as a radio operator in the German Mercantile Marine Service, and helped to embezzle the dole office when on Social Welfare Benefits. His mother Ethel owned several houses in Milkwood Road, which she rented to the down-and-outs of Brixton, making a tidy living in the process. Her husband, my grandfather, died shortly after my father's birth in 1922 as a direct result of the mustard gas he inhaled when fighting in the Great War of 1914–18. He was also a champion boxer and had a number of titles under his belt.

Ethel became an extremely dominating widow who always wore black, even in the heat of summer. Her control over Victor was in some strange way insidious, with her doting love for her young son going beyond what many people would consider normal. She detested his girlfriends, especially my mother, who took refuge in Milkwood Road after she discovered she had become pregnant with my elder sister, Linda. There were constant vicious screaming matches between them that led my mother to return to her abusive father time after time. The rows persisted long after Ethel's death, as the same kind of accusations were often repeated, both orally and with violence, escalating my mother's taunts at Victor's love for his mother to violent and often uncontrollable heights as I hid under the dining room table.

At the age of fourteen, Victor left school and went to work as an apprentice to a local baker, a position Ethel had found for him in the bakery opposite their house in Milkwood Road, Herne Hill. When Victor was sixteen, a benevolent aunt passed away, leaving Victor a small inheritance to be used for his education and it was decided that he should join His Majesty's Merchant Navy, far less risky that being in the firing line. So off to Southampton he went, following a year-long bout of scarlet fever which, along with polio, was prevalent in those days. Some good came out of it as, during the time he was ill, he taught himself to read. The funds enabled Victor to enrol at naval college and provided him with a uniform and, at long last, an identity that would to some degree shape the rest of his life.

World War Two was imminent and Victor's life was about to start its out-of-control ride. On his first voyage as a junior ranking trainee radio operator, his ship was torpedoed by a Japanese submarine in the Pacific, not far from Korea. His crowded life raft floated for several days in the open sea until they were all saved by a Dutch freight carrier. Only then, after three days, was he able to urinate. Perhaps the full warped reality and the shock of being torpedoed had set in. The event undoubtedly affected Victor, from his teenage years right up until his death in 1994. His survival confirmed his belief in a new superman, born to be better than indestructible. He often told me he would be "a legend," and think he is probably as close as we could get to one. He later served under a number of flags including the Panamanian one, working on ships which were running illegal arms, gun-running ships headed for every dodgy port that would unload the illicit cargo. These ships always ran a skeleton crew, as the work was far too dangerous for a normal rational crew.

After his return to Milkwood Road, my father married his first wife, Daphne; a woman always in the background of my family life, since Daphne and Victor had a child, a boy named Neil, my half-brother, who I never saw or met.

Domestic Fraud

Whenever Victor's fantasy world was challenged he would resort to violence. Not in defence, but in an act to regain power over reality. On paper, he claimed to have ten children in order to claim tax-relief and child benefits and devised forged identities for each. He created several phantom families, some with disabled children, and set up bank accounts for each. He used a variety of different identities. If there was a social welfare benefit to be had, he would have it. Apparently there are various characteristics that are often contained in fraudulent claims of this type – fictitious children are often twins or disabled, including the claimant themselves, and that's one of the warning signals civil servants look for when they become suspicious. Victor waged war on the benefit system until he was discovered, and when he was discovered there was only one thing left he could do, and that was to turn his frustration and fury on me.

The Trial

The trial was held in Court No. 1 at the Old Bailey, where Mr Brian Leary, council for the prosecution, told the jury that Victor was "a menace to children and society." Victor had forged letters and altered real ones. He had changed the meaning of words and defaced them. *Not*, now read *now*, and *un*, as in *unlikely*, had been deleted so that the word became *likely*. The letters were palimpsests, pieces of writing where the meaning of the original had been effaced to make room for later writing, later meanings, but still had traces remaining of the originals. Leary didn't know it at the time but he had identified something few others had, an insight into my father's mind and, as the case progressed, Victor gained a psychological profile of a serial fraudster. Identity defines meaning and Victor's trial for false identity offered a glimpse into the oneiric world of a man who avoided identity. The judge was desperate to capture something he assumed all men had – an identity. He thought he could punish Victor by using a mirror of reality, a reflection of truth.

Evidence for Victor's conviction included forged academic certificates, fake Masters and a PhD from a non-existent university in San Diego, purchased from an ad in the back pages of *Exchange & Mart* selling bogus degrees from dodgy printers in Peckham. A platter of photocopied documents claiming that he was a Fellow of The Royal Society, a Fellow of The Society of

Arts, a Fellow of The Royal Astronomical Society, all gained by deception and altered to suit his purpose, a purpose greater than the crime of which he was convicted. Victor was a man who fantasised a life more exciting, more glamorous, more anything than his own. He made his own life that of someone else, a patchwork hero, and in the process completely lost his own identity while trying to make an identity – an illusive identity that diminished his own. Indeed, so deep was this twist of reality that the judge had doubts about Victor's sanity and engaged a police surgeon to give an expert opinion. Victor returned to his holding cell along Dead Man's Walk, a narrow passage through which prisoners passed to and from their courtroom appearances, and where under the flagstones executed prisoners were buried. He thought of the remorse those souls must feel; remorse because they, like he, were innocent by comparison to many. The Old Bailey must be full of ghosts.

The Right Honourable John Maude of The Old Bailey made a recommendation for Victor's psychological appraisal but failed to have Victor sectioned. Three psychiatrists were consulted; two corroborated, but the third forgot to file his report. Although it was evident from Victor's obsessive-compulsive disorder that he was psychotic, rather than sending him to the loony bin, off to prison Victor went.

Defence council Mr Edward Grayson could only offer a comic portrayal of Victor as a "Walter Mitty character," a "harmless nuisance" in a society where much bigger problems loomed. He placed the greater blame on the Greater London Council for employing Victor and accepting his fake references with open arms, without the rigorous police checks we have today.

Grayson used James Thurber's short story, *The Secret Life Of Walter Mitty*, aptly. It had recently been made into a movie starring comedian Danny Kaye and was popular at that time. Many, possibly even the Judge, had seen it. Walter Mitty was an ineffectual person who indulged in fantastic daydreams of personal triumphs. But in truth Victor was the contrast to Danny Kay's loveable warped version. Victor had a darker, capricious soul of violence and insanity. Grayson had identified something, and once identified, the monster could be slain. The simplicity of Walter Mitty disarmed deeper scrutiny. Walter was Victor's second given name, Victor Walter Charles Biddlecome, later to be changed by deed-poll to Victor Walter Charles Lionheart-Richardson, and then later, on his release from prison, to that of Lionheart-Riechardson in a vain attempt to evade his prison record, his real identity.

Cuba

Cuba was sympathetic to its African commanders and was happy to supply its communist brothers with arms. Its leader, Fidel Castrol, felt duty-bound to send troops to Africa, not only to secure the payment owed him for the arms shipment, but also to put on a show of support for his communist comrades and defiance to the United Nations, so he sent a ship to Africa manned by soldiers he called his "Internationalists."

The truth was that the Cubans' voyage from Mariel to the

Congolese coast took 23 days. The 3,000 troops were never allowed above deck for fear of detection by American aerial intelligence. The troops were quartered in the cargo holds that had been used for shipping raw sugar. Seasickness, vomiting and unsuccessful attempts to adjust to stiflingly hot, cramped and nauseating conditions aboard the ex-sugar freighter made it hell. The vessel arrived off the Congolese coast and the troops began the welcome debarkation from the ships at Pointe Noir around midnight. The Cuban expeditionary force was not there to launch a revolution, but to collect diamonds and the arms shipment it thought had been delivered. Instead, it became embroiled in the UN battle of Elizabethville and was defeated on all sides.

Despite conflicting justifications, the Cuban intervention played well to domestic audiences in Cuba and Fidel's stature improved internationally as he attempted to re-establish himself as the philosophical and martial leader of revolutionary movements throughout the Third World, at a cost of over a thousand men. On 2 December 2005, an ageing Fidel Castro addressed his involvement in his last personally delivered speech during the Revolutionary Armed Forces Day in Havana. In it he said: "Never before had a Third World country acted to support another people in armed conflict, such as Africa, beyond its own geographical neighbourhood!"

Victor's Diary
During his captivity in Elizabethville, Victor kept a notebook of loose A4 paper. The following is my transcript of this. In it, he

suggests that he was involved in two battles, not just one, and that during the second he was already under house arrest, for reasons that remain unclear. In his footnote, he feels compelled to write, *The author of this first person article is now studying medicine through London University, England.* Even in his statement of fact, the truth it serves is to no avail…

26*th* December 1962

I SERVED IN THE PENAL BATTALION OF PRESIDENT TSHOMBE'S SOUTHERN COMMAND.

Nine weeks ago I was in the city of Boudonville in charge of the Northern army command, having been personally appointed by President Tshombe in Elizabethville. I was decorated with the Katangese Legion of Honour, and Croix de Guerre. (Who would have thought it, a simple boy like me from Brixton, unbelievable really.)

In Boudouinville, I opened a hospital which had remained closed for two years after the Belgians had withdrawn from the Congo. With the help of my Grays Medical Dictionary, I treated some several hundred cases over five months. When my identity was disclosed as a fake, a white mercenaries' military court sat in judgement on me and stripped me of my rank of colonel. (I was gutted!) I was ordered out of Katanga to Portuguese Angola, but after my court martial I was flown to a military transport prison in Southern Katanga, a place called Fort Kasapa, and held in detention. I couldn't believe it when they asked me to treat casualties requiring medical attention.

I was the only white man in the military prison at Fort Kasapa, eighteen miles from the city of Elizabethville and capital of Katanga. The commandant of the military prison ordered me to be sent to him and under escort, he's a real bastard. In French, he informed me that mercenaries were based several miles outside the United Nations base at Elizabethville, and that an attack on the United Nations was about to take place to force and break out of the encircling ring.

Fort Kasapa was a 'Beau Geste' kind of place, really; it even had the motto, 'Death For All Who Serve'. I suppose he picked me because I was the only person who had stitched people back together. You might even say that I was the only medically experienced person in the military prison, therefore I took what precautions I could. I was told to serve and remain at my post whatever happened or else the arsehole would shoot me. The military prison at Fort Kasapa had been built by the Belgians as a military fort, its outer walls were some fifteen feet in height and the base some four feet thick; into the walls some massive steel gates had been added. This was to be the second bloodbath I had experienced out here in this shit hole. It was like I could see a red light flashing in front of me but there was no escape, but deep in my heart I knew I was a living lie, you know, it was like death was sharpening his scythe for a ripe harvest. Early next morning, just after four, I was aroused by the sound of military equipment. Several units of white mercenaries had been instructed in the night to come back to Fort Kasapa. Katangese Gendarmarie were re-grouping with our battalion, death was surely smiling and I felt excited, even exhilarated by it. That night there was very little moon, it was pitch black. The sky was heavy and overcast as it was the rainy season in central Africa. The surrounding jungle was black and seemed omniscient with silence. I prayed that night, for I was a coward and afraid. I asked God to save me so I could go to Milkwood Road and see my mum again.

Just after 06.00am on the 28th December, our radio operator listened in on the Canadian Signal Corp. He informed us that the United Nations had attacked the front line of defence and were now advancing on us. A helicopter ventured above my head and was pounded with shells. It never stood a chance in that hell of fire, it went down in the jungle, breaking up as it went. There was something in the smell of that which clings to me to this day, makes me feel sick. I wake up sometimes in the early hours remembering and dripping sweat.

Gunfire followed by mortar shells exploding. I saw the remains of men I knew falling around me. All hell broke loose. A low-flying jet passed over us and our anti-aircraft positions chattered, barked and coughed, it was just like a film but real. A second, then third jet crossed our sights. After that I lost count but I know we hit several of them. Then there was a Godalmighty explosion as the main building was hit several times by mortar and erupted in flames. My hospital received several direct hits and the smell of burning flesh produced a smoke that made it difficult to breathe, so I ordered my staff down into the storerooms of the fort, where I closed my eyes and hid.

By now, the intense anti-aircraft fire of the attacks by the United Nations planes dominated all sense of hearing. All colours, white, brown and black, fell dead. There was no distinguishing touch for those that fell.

I need to put on record that I couldn't do much. I mentally signed death certificates as the stock of morphine I had prepared several weeks previously quickly diminished. I had no drugs to kill pain itself. I don't know when, but I too had been injured by a piece of flying shrapnel.

My stomach was aching, streaming blood near my navel. I saw a deep incision and felt sick. I was afraid. I did not want to die, at least not like this. The blood would not stop so I stitched myself up before the pain wave hit me.

An hour or so passed and that's when I saw General Samuel disappearing into the jungle. After that, I was asked by the Katangese to surrender – they just gave up. They asked me because I was the only white man left to talk to the English-speaking Swedish United Nations troops who were gathered outside the fort. I made my way to the main gates, mounted one of the lookout towers, and waved a hastily made white flag in surrender. I was a hero!

* * *

— Chapter Photos —

About Martin Richardson

After leaving South Croxted, Martin Richardson eventually enrolled as a degree student at Middlesex Polytechnic and gained the world's first PhD in Display Holography from The Royal College of Art in 1988. In 1999 he was awarded the Millennium Fellowship by the UK Millennium Government Commission and in 2002 the prestigious American Shearwater Foundation Award for Achievements in Holographic Art. In 2009 he became an Associate to the Royal Photographic Society and awarded the Saxby Medal for his contributions to 3-D imaging. He is currently Professor of Modern Holography at De Montfort University, Leicester, where he leads Holographic Research.

Lightning Source UK Ltd.
Milton Keynes UK
UKOW03072825l112

202744UK00001B/3/P